Habit Busting

A 10-step plan that will change your life

Pete Cohen and Sten Cummins
with Jennai Cox

Thorsons

This book is dedicated to the lovely, gorgeous Vanessa Corley.

Pete Cohen (2001)

I would especially like to thank (in order of appearance):
Robert Anton Wilson for your inspirational curiosity and the book Prometheus Rising.
Michelle Cornell for your advice and encouragement.
Michael Breen for your wise council and patient, yet hilarious tuition.
Laura Nolan and Mach, without you this book would never have happened.
Dr Richard Bandler the genius who created Neuro Linguistic Programming, the thinking
that enables freedom.
Paul McKenna the most charming PR man the human brain ever had.
Shelly Loughney for your strong words softly spoken.
Pete Cohen, the wisest clown in toy town.
Special thanks to Jennai Cox, without whom this book would be very different, and may
never have made it into print.
Thank you all.

Sten Cummins (2001)

Thorsons
An Imprint of HarperCollins*Publishers*
77–85 Fulham Palace Road
Hammersmith
London W6 8JB

The Thorsons website address is: www.thorsons.com

and *Thorsons*

are trademarks of HarperCollins*Publishers* Limited

Published by Thorsons 2002

10 9 8 7 6 5 4 3 2 1

© Pete Cohen and Sten Cummins 2002

Pete Cohen and Sten Cummins assert the moral right
to be identified as the authors of this work

A catalogue record for this book is
available from the British Library

ISBN 0 7225 4009 4

Printed and bound in Great Britain by
Martins the Printers Ltd, Berwick upon Tweed

Contents

Foreword

Pete Cohen's ability to help people transcend their unwanted habits, fears and phobias is amazing. Last year I worked with Pete on an innovative week-long series for GMTV called *House of Fear*. The aim of the series was to help four people who all had debilitating fears and phobias. These people's physical, mental and emotional responses were tested and proved beyond doubt that their fears and phobias were socially handicapping them and stopping them from living normal lives.

I had my doubts that these people could really change in such a short period of time. Pete worked with them for three days and when I saw them again on the fourth day, the results were astounding. I watched as once again these people were exposed to their deepest fears. However, this time their reactions had changed from panic and terror to complete control. These people were cured of their unwanted behaviour, and were experiencing a new sense of confidence, control and a determined conviction to enjoy their lives more.

I would recommend Pete Cohen and the processes in this book to anyone who wishes to break or bust any unwanted habits or behaviour. With his methods, so very much is possible. Freedom from anxiety or terror is within their grasp, here in the pages of the book.

Dr Hilary Jones, M.B.B.S.
GP and media doctor

Introduction

My name is Pete Cohen and I have been helping people bust their habits for over 10 years.

I have always found human behaviour fascinating, and through my explorations and experiences of working with thousands of people I have become convinced that the majority of people can overcome their limiting habits. Habits are quite simply things we have learned, whether it be smoking, low self-esteem, nail-biting or fear of flying. They are thoughts, behaviours and actions that we have practised over time.

The Habit-busting techniques and strategies in this book will help you to unlearn your bad habits and replace them with more productive and enjoyable ways of living your life. You will learn how to make simple but highly effective changes, and ultimately you will gain more control and become freer and happier.

What You Will Need for This Book

Winning starts with beginning.
Robert Schuller

In the course of reading this book we want you to become an investigator rather than a critic. To do this all you will need are an inquisitive and open mind, a notebook and a pen. Please give yourself time to change: you have worked hard at creating these habits and need the time you deserve to bring about change.

In the work that we do, we start out by reminding each person of four absolute truths:

1. Every human being has positive worth. That worth is non-negotiable. Your worth is always there, and it's always going to be there, in spite of the behaviours and habits you may have picked up during your life, and however appropriate or inappropriate they may be. Nothing that happens in life can change that.

2. Other people's reactions to what you do and say are just that – other people's reactions. Their reactions, comments and attitudes are theirs, not yours. The only person who can define you is you. You are not responsible for how other people feel about you.

3. When you make a decision, you invariably make the best decision you can at that time, with the options you believe you have. There is a positive intention motivating all your behaviour. However the behaviour might seem with the benefit of hindsight, all behaviour is positive in intent.

4. Every person has within them all of the strengths and resources necessary to change into the person they want to be.

List of Habits This Book Can Help You Break

Smoking	Drinking	Drugs dependency
Overweight	Nail-biting	Eating disorders
Gambling	Being stressed	Inability to relax
Worrying too much	Road rage	Being pessimistic
Procrastinating	Problems with	Low self-confidence
Negative thinking	people	Feeling like a loser
Feeling guilty		

step 1

What Are Habits?

No one was born with low self-esteem, no one was born with an eating disorder and no one was born biting their nails, stressed or with a tendency to procrastinate. All habits are behaviours we have learned and practised so often that they have become second nature. And because they are part of our *second* nature, and not our first, we are closer to our true selves without them. We only feel that they are a part of us because we have practised them for so long and are conditioned to have them. We often end up feeling that they are who we are. They are not.

Like many of the other essential skills we learn as we grow, such as talking, eating and walking, habits are behaviours learned by watching others and copying them because these habits appear to make others look good and/or feel good. The motivation to learn is no different: we believe we are smoking/eating more/compulsively cleaning/procrastinating in our own best interests – to make ourselves happy. So we practise these behaviours, believing that they will not only make us feel better about, but also think better of, ourselves, and help to make a reality of the person we think we would like to be.

A Positive Intention

Through our work with people who wish to break habits, we have come to believe that behind all behaviour is a positive intention. The brain only ever suggests a behaviour it thinks is the best and most effective way of making us feel better, and it has learned what makes us feel better or more comfortable from our behaviour in the past.

Because we are fast learners, habits develop and become fixed very quickly. Take smoking, for example. We watch people smoking and because it looks cool we think it is an appropriate and useful way to behave. We are driven to do it, even though it is hard and it hurts. How many people enjoy their first cigarette? Yet they go through the pain of smoking in order to be like other people. The association of smoking with cool is learned and becomes hard-wired in our brains so that smoking equals cool.

People do not have habits for the sake of it. Their brain suggests to them what it thinks is best or what in the past might have alleviated some discomfort or seemed attractive. So whenever we feel discomfort, the brain kicks in to relieve us by suggesting what by past repetition it has been taught makes us feel better, even when we know it no longer works.

In the 1940s, behavioural psychologist B F Skinner built two mazes, one for rats and another for a group of graduates. As an incentive to find the centre he placed in the middle of the first some chocolate and in the second some $10 bills. The rats and graduates ran around the mazes until they found the reward. When the chocolate was removed from the first maze, the rats no longer showed any interest in finding the centre of the maze. The graduates, however, would still run through the maze in search of the middle, even when they knew there was no longer any money there. The habit, once established, continued even when the reason for doing it had been removed.

Pete writes: When I was young we had a pet dog, and of course I got used to having it around. I would see it all the time and it would come whenever I called out its name. Even though the dog died almost a decade ago, whenever I visit my parents I still expect him to be there, running to greet me. This demonstrates conditioned behaviour; the pattern is similar to the way in which many habits develop and are sustained. Even though we try to break them, the brain keeps on suggesting them. Because we have spent so much time doing them, the brain persists in urging us that familiar behaviours are still best.

What about other behaviours? Well, when some people are in a room full of strangers feeling uncomfortable, for example, their brain may suggest smoking because that is what has habitually made them feel more at ease. Although some of those who are fat want to lose weight, their brain still suggests food when they feel uncomfortable, because eating has for many years always made them feel better. Others may find biting their nails brings comfort when they feel uncomfortable or find themselves in an awkward situation. Because the behaviour has worked before to alleviate discomfort in each of these hypothetical situations, the brain has learned to see it as a solution and suggests it whenever any feelings of discomfort arise. The behaviour becomes a habit.

At the time we begin to cultivate a habit, we are merely obeying the brain's tendency to make us behave in a way that it believes is best for us. Think about this: if eating a sweet takes your attention away from the pain of falling over often enough when you are young, the brain can become conditioned to suggest eating something sweet whenever we experience discomfort.

We go on practising whichever habit it is we have learned to the point where we are so good at it that we don't really have to think about it any more. So skilled do we become at putting things off, biting our nails or feeling stressed or guilty that we fail to realize these behaviours no longer serve even a perceived useful purpose. We get to the stage where we are merely going through the motions of a behaviour out of no more than habit. Some of us still enjoy our habits, although not always the feeling we're left with afterwards.

During the Second World War, a number of Japanese garrisons were sent to occupy and guard little islands in the Pacific. They were instructed to shoot at invaders or enemies of Japan. With no radio contact, they refused to accept, even long after the fact, that the war was over. Every day they continued to don their uniforms, clean their weapons and wait for 'enemy' ships to pass, and they would shoot at them. A number of these garrisons were still being found well into the 1970s – discovered because they were shooting at fishing boats. Instead of rushing in to instruct the soldiers to stop fighting, a former sergeant in the Japanese army, wearing his old uniform, was sent to the island. He thanked the men and, after speaking to them at length, informed them that the war was over. Their conditioned behaviour could now be replaced by actions and experiences more in keeping with the outside world.

This story illustrates well how humans behave. We act in ways that are no longer useful, continuing because we have no way of knowing that we have a choice about how to behave. But we have.

Ask yourself this: do you think you have a choice when deciding whether or not to accept your brain's instructions?

You have, and you are not limited to doing what you have always done in the past.

With the will to change and an openness to change comes the realization that your choices are limitless.

Like the approach used by the sergeant in the story, this book is here to coach, support and hold your hand as you make positive changes. It is not going to get cross or impatient with you, nor laugh at or bully you into making changes. We understand what you need to do and the process you need to go through. We are not going to tell you that you *have* to change or *should* change. All we are saying is that you *can* change. The choice is entirely up to you.

> People's minds are like parachutes – they only function when they are open.
>
> *Leanne Hastie*

> The most powerful thing you can do to change the world, is to change your own beliefs about the nature of life, people, reality, to something more positive ... and begin to act accordingly.
>
> *Shakti Gawain, Creative Visualization*

Time for Something New

What happens when you become so good at something, whether it is a hobby or a way of carrying out your work, that it ceases to hold your interest or drive your motivation?

Most people look for a new challenge.

Well, seeing as you are now so good at your habit, the challenge could be to find something else which you can become just as skilled at.

So many people do not even realize that this choice is available to them.

Whose Fault?

It has been suggested that, unlike many of the other creatures who inhabit the Earth, the human race is still evolving. A cockroach has always been a cockroach, but over many thousands of years humans have evolved into what we are today. We are the newest species on the planet. Do you think we are also the most intelligent? Think about what we are particularly good at: evolving, surviving, inventing, destroying, criticizing, inflicting pain, hating, killing. Perhaps we are not as intelligent as we like to think.

The ways in which we learn contribute to this apparent lack of greater human intelligence. As babies and children we absorb almost everything that happens around us, soaking up everything like a sponge. We have no specific mechanism with which to filter the incoming information; we just watch and learn particular behaviours without knowing at the time which are useful and which not.

Having habits is, in some ways, not entirely our own fault, and because we are a species that is still evolving (in other words, still imperfect), we should expect to have imperfections. Adopting, practising and having habits is part of our imperfect human make-up. This is not to excuse habits, just a way of explaining how humans have come to have them. Before we go any further, let's just accept that habits are

Stop looking for a scapegoat in your life but be willing to face the truth within yourself and right your own wrongs.

Eileen Caddy,
Footprints on the
Path

something we bring upon ourselves, even though this is in many cases unintentional. You might like to blame someone else or some particular set of circumstances – something you say to yourself, something you picture or something you feel before you find yourself engaging in the habit – but you have control. You have a lot more control than you probably think.

A client of ours who had successfully conquered his tendency to overeat continued to attend a support group for overeaters once a week for fear he would lapse back into his old ways. At the beginning of each session he had to stand up and say 'Hello, I am Colin, and I am an overeater.' When we asked him one day about the last time he had actually overeaten, Colin said that it had been more than five years, but that he often felt a strong urge to do so. 'So, you tell yourself every week that you are something that you have not been for more than five years?' we asked. 'Do you realize the amount of control you really have?' At the next meeting of his group, he decided to change his opening mantra to, 'Hello, I am Colin, and I am in control.' The group leader told Colin in no uncertain terms that he was not in control, and he was asked to leave the group. It was almost as though Colin was being told that he could never have control over his eating and needed to hang on to his problem instead of getting over it and getting on with his life.

Cracking the Code

This is not a book that is going to show you how to stop overeating or stop smoking or stop being late. There are plenty of such books already on the shelves. While they may

I now can let go of worn-out conditions and worn-out ideas.

help, they also reinforce the very behaviour you're trying to overcome. If you buy a book about how to give up cigarettes, for example, what do you think you will almost constantly be thinking about all the time? This book is going to show you how to crack the code of habits, once and for all.

Two monks on a long walk come to a stretch of water. Nearby stands a beautiful woman who asks for help getting across. The younger of the two lifts her up and carries her over the water, then goes back and resumes his walk with the elder monk. After a few minutes the young monk detects a sense of agitation and annoyance in the older monk, and asks him what is wrong. 'We are not allowed to look at or touch, let alone carry women,' the older monk tells him. The young monk replies: 'I put her down on the other side of the water; you are still carrying her.'

How people think and learn is the same code by which their habit or habits are formed. Once you know how to crack the code of your own thought processes, you will be able to use what you find for the rest of your life in solving problems, thinking creatively, and more. You will start to notice how you approach issues in your life. Often, just this awareness can help you experiment with a different approach. Instead of allowing what has failed and what you no longer want to consume your thoughts, start right now by thinking about what it is you *do* want.

The individual who wants to reach the top in business must appreciate the might of the force of habit – and must understand that practices are what create habits. He must be quick to break those habits that can break him and hasten to adopt those practices to achieve the success he desires.

Paul Getty

What Is the Difference between a Good and a Bad Habit?

We do not have to label habits good or bad. Just accept them for what they are. Most people are well aware what any particular habit does to them or for them. In many cases we can become good at habits, but can eventually feel bad about them. They make us feel either better or worse than the person we want to be. Perhaps the difference between a good and a bad habit for each person is whether they want to go on doing it.

A 'bad' habit, such as feeling stressed, might not in itself necessarily be bad. The first time we feel stressed, it might not make us feel bad or be very bad for us at all. But then, if the stressful feeling becomes ingrained as a habit, our brain acts as though it is still the best way for us to behave, and we go on doing it.

Take procrastinating, the art of putting things off. It is something that many people with habits do – in other words, they postpone trying to break them. People who procrastinate often spend so much time planning to put things off that they fail to realize how much better they would feel if they just did them and got them out of the way.

Your first challenge will be to stop deferring action and beginning to take some.

When the basketball player Michael Jordan was asked to throw the ball and miss the basket in an American TV commercial, he couldn't do it. The film crew had to do about 20 takes before they got the shot they wanted. Why? For so long had Jordan practised the good habit of getting the ball into the net, he found it

**impossible to miss deliberately. The behaviour of scoring success-
fully had become hard-wired in his brain.**

Bad habits could be regarded as those we want to be rid of.
They are bad because, even though we might feel great
while engaging in them, afterwards we feel terrible. They are
bad because we no longer want to have them in our lives,
and it makes us sad to believe we always will. Part of this
belief stems from how we acquire the habits in the first place,
and how we have dealt with them over time.

How We Acquire Habits

So, a habit is a behaviour repeated so often we can practise
it without thinking. In other words, it is a type of self-
conditioning. People are conditioning themselves all the
time. Anyone who has worked in an office will be familiar with
the regular discussions revolving around what to eat, what
not to eat, what was or wasn't eaten for breakfast and how
much should or should not have been eaten or drunk the
night before. And so it goes on. People sit around in front of
computers every day and condition themselves and each
other into putting on weight.

We condition ourselves throughout our lives – and adver-
tisers in particular take huge advantage of this: 'A Mars a
day helps you work, rest and play'; 'Have a break, have a
Kitkat.' 'Carlsberg, probably the best lager in the world.'
Beans means what? Heinz? Do they really?

We are also influenced to think in certain ways, to link certain behaviours with particular times and places (a coffee
and a cigarette; tea and biscuits), and habits develop

The way to change the world is to change your attitude towards it, not just once, but all the time.

because we have conditioned ourselves into adopting and practising these behaviours. They are comforting, and the behaviours come to feel like part of us. Because the idea of change has failed to take hold in the past, we condition ourselves into believing that it never can.

When asked why they cannot give up their habits, most people we have worked with say it is because they have had them for so long. Well, does that mean they are doomed to have them for ever? We develop habits through practice and repetition, so imagining life without them can seem difficult.

Attitude is the mind's paintbrush, it can colour any situation.

What if we can change the way we think about our attitudes towards our behaviour, as well as the behaviour itself? Elite athletes, drug addicts and overeaters have more in common in terms of how they think than at first appears. Whereas the athlete will ask herself: 'What can I do today that will make my performance better for tomorrow?', the drug addict might ask: 'Where will I get my fix today?' and the overeater might say: 'What sugary, fattening, comforting foods can I eat today?' All of these people are highly motivated, but their motivation takes them in widely varying directions.

The athlete believes she can always get better, and makes the necessary changes to her diet or training programme. The overeater or drug addict hold no such self-belief, and so behave as though they will either always be fat or always be an addict. Each feels so hooked on his habit that even the desire to change is not enough. But whether we are aware of it or not, we can take ourselves in whatever direction we want to go.

The Three-word Success Course

Everything you need to know about success can be reduced to three simple words:

> Can
>
> Will
>
> Now

Can

Can you do it? Do you possess the innate ability? The truth is: Yes! Think about the times you have got over things in the past. You have the same innate ability as Shakespeare, Einstein, Marie Curie, Martha Graham and George Washington Carver. They were not born with any more raw talent than you. You have powers buried deep inside you that you haven't discovered yet. You probably do not even realize just how amazing you really are.

Will

Will you use your remarkable ability? Just because you can does not necessarily mean you will. You have the same raw ability as a Shakespeare, but what did Shakespeare do that you haven't done yet? Through remarkable effort and perseverance, Shakespeare gained access to his remarkable ability. Will you?

Now

When will you begin? Many people die with their best songs unsung. Don't wait; use your remarkable ability NOW.

How Our Brains Work

The good news is that because of the way the brain works, big changes can happen fast. We can spend months and months trying to make small changes, but they will occur only very slowly. If we make a big, dramatic gesture, change happens instantly.

A psychiatrist called Ramashandra once worked with some people who, despite having lost limbs, still experienced what is known as 'phantom pain' in the part of the body they had lost. The pain was in many cases excruciating, and every other type of therapy had, over many years, failed to bring any sort of relief. Ramashandra worked with one man who wanted relief from what felt like a permanently clenched fist. In reality he had no hand to make a fist with. No matter what therapy he'd tried or what drug was injected the man could not lose the sensation that his fist was clenched. Ramashandra got the man to place his good hand and his other wrist into a box. Because of the way in which a mirror had been placed inside, when the man looked through the top of the box he saw not just one, but two hands. This tricked the man's brain into believing he could unclench the missing hand, which he did. Once this man's internal representation of his condition had been addressed, the problem was solved.

The brain works in a way that it believes will keep us feeling good, and we start learning how to feel good as children.

Pete writes: I remember falling over in a playground when I was a child and being taken into a little room by a teacher where, on a shelf, was a train. In each carriage was a different type of sweet – jelly beans, chocolate buttons and so on. I was given a sweet and immediately my attention was taken away from the pain of falling over. My friends soon got wind of this and they all started falling over on purpose. I even remember smearing the blood from some- one else's knee on to my arm, to get back to the sweets room. In this way, from a very early age, I learned to associate the dissolu- tion of pain with eating something sweet. A neurological pathway formed in my brain which equated the solution to pain with eating a sweet. My brain learned that whenever I felt pain, I got a sweet. Even years later, whenever I fell and hurt myself, I would crave something sweet.

That is how most associations come about. We learn them in one particular set of circumstances and repeat them when- ever we find ourselves in a similar situation. A behaviour or pattern of thinking is established, so whenever we are in a similar situation the brain suggests the solution it thinks best. People go along with the brain's 'advice' because it is familiar, comforting and something they believe will be good for them.

Some people who want to change become preoccupied with wanting to find out why they developed a certain habit in the first place. 'Why' is not the issue; getting on with change is.

Reprogramming

In order to change a habit, we need to reprogramme our brains. Are you going to rely on cigarettes, alcohol or drugs for the rest of your life? Instead of smoking, overeating or biting our nails because it might help you to feel better (tem- porarily), you need to build new neurological pathways in the brain to tell you that another kind of behaviour – say, going for a walk, lying down for 10 minutes, or doing something

The impossible is often the untried.
Jim Goodwin

else that gives you pleasure – will make you feel just as good, if not better. We need to repeat the new behaviour until the old way of thinking withers and is forgotten.

Are you always going to rely on your habit to control you? Will you allow cigarettes, drugs, food or stress to get the better of you for ever? Are you going to carry on giving yourself a hard time? Or are you going to change?

Exercise

1   Get a notebook and three different coloured pens.
2   From the following list, underline in one colour the habits you want to stop.
3   In another colour, underline those you are happy with.
4   With the last colour, underline those habits you wish to adopt.

As you read through this list, bear in mind that all of these habits are simply things you have *learned* or can learn how to do.

Cleaning your teeth	Smoking
Eating fruit and vegetables	Procrastinating
Nail-biting	Overeating
Taking regular exercise	Laughing regularly
Relaxing	Taking plenty of sleep
Washing and bathing	Listening to people
Getting stressed	Taking drugs
Gambling	Eating slowly

Getting drunk

Having low self-esteem

Spending time with friends

Cooking

Wearing clean clothes

Enjoying a hobby

Gardening

Getting angry

Giving yourself a hard time

Eating slowly

Eating too fast

Drinking water

Brushing your hair

Kissing

Now, in your notebook make a list of the habits you've underlined which you'd like to break. For each of these, answer the questions below.

1 Were you born with this habit?
2 Did you learn this habit?
3 Is it an adopted habit, i.e., one that you remember either your parents or friends having?
4 Are you good at this habit?
5 Is this habit good for you?
6 Will this habit serve you well in the future?
7 Do you want to change it?
8 Are you prepared to change?
9 What do you need to change?
10 What is it about you that will help you to change?

Many people think change is difficult. They have been conditioned to believe that. But think of all the other times in your life when you've changed. The clothes you wear, the places you go, the things you talk about are probably vastly different now from what they were 10 years ago. You made a transition, and going back to your past wardrobe, past hangouts or past conversations is unthinkable, maybe even unbearable. In many of these instances the change you made was not a struggle. The changes occurred consciously or even unconsciously, without tears, fuss or effort.

Central HQ

The brain is the nerve centre or headquarters of the body. It processes information coming in about what is going on around and inside us, it makes complex comparisons and decisions, and it issues instructions to the rest of the body. The brain is also responsible for the regulation of emotions such as pleasure, anger, fear, relaxation and sociability, and sensations such as hunger, thirst, pain, nausea, etc., as well as memory and learning.

All this is possible because of the way in which the brain is made up of a network of millions of tiny nerve cells. These make lots of connections with other nerve cells, which fire off huge numbers of messages to each other at great speed, just like very complicated electrical circuits.

However, until very recently the traditional view among scientists was that no new brain cells could be added to the human brain during adulthood, no matter what we learned or experienced. The brain was considered to be unlike most other tissues in the body, in which cells are continually being replaced throughout life. This view has been eroded gradually, particularly during the last decade, as evidence has accumulated that new brain cells are produced during our lives. In 1998, researchers working under the direction of Professor Fred H Gage at the Salk Institute of Biological

Studies in California and at the Sahlgrenska University Hospital in Göteborg, Sweden, discovered that large numbers of new brain cells develop in an area of the brain involved with learning and memory.

This suggests completely new ways of explaining how the mind carries out its functions. Research is continuing around the world to corroborate these findings and to establish whether other regions of the brain behave in the same way. So far the results look very encouraging, and the data suggest that learning stimulates the development of new brain cells, which reinforces the 'use it or lose it' theory of brain ageing.

All this is still very new and may be controversial, and a great deal more work still needs to be done, but the findings increase the likelihood that our experiences throughout adulthood can actually alter the structure of the brain. Pretty well all the theories about learning and memory contend that modifications at the junctions between brain cells produce memories. Now it seems possible that the development of new circuitry in the brain may also play a role in memory. Researchers are emphasizing that we still do not know for sure what these new cells do, but it looks as though we may have more control over our own brains than we thought.

This is, of course, great news for anyone who wants to change some of their own thought patterns or behaviours. It suggests that we do not have to remain passively with what we have got, that we do not need to be victims of the way we are made. This naturally does not include medical conditions; they always require expert medical examination and treatment. But for everyday activities it appears as though we might actually have the capacity to change the circuitry in our brains by learning and practising changes in our behaviour or the way we think.

If you really want to change your habits, you can. Keep your changes in mind and you can change your mind.

If you can't change your mind, are you sure you still have one?

Robert Heinlein

The Mind/Body Connection

Your body follows what your mind tells it to do. How many of your everyday thoughts are new, and how many are old ones you have been carrying around for as long as you can remember? Each time you repeat a thought, you reinforce its power; the circuit or pathway along which you think it gets stronger, leaving less room for new and empowering, creative ideas.

Now think about what you take in during an average day. If you mix with people who are depressed or talk constantly about their problems, there is a strong chance that your own feelings will start to mirror theirs. On the other hand, if you mingle with successful people who talk enthusiastically about their plans for the future, you will feel very differently about yourself and the world in general.

Desperate to meet his guru, a Buddhist follower climbs a series of mountains and walks for many days overland until at last he comes face to face with the man who has inspired his beliefs. As soon as he arrives, the follower starts talking about himself and his life, almost without stopping, until the guru intercedes to offer him a cup of tea. Somewhat taken aback at having been interrupted, the follower nevertheless accepts. As he resumes his dialogue, the guru begins to pour the tea, and carries on pouring until the cup is overflowing and tea is pouring off the table and on to the follower's legs. 'What are you doing?' he asks, as the hot water burns his knees. 'Can you not see that you are just like the tea cup?' says the guru. 'You are so full of all the things you think you need that there is no room for anything new.'

Life is full and overflowing with the new. But it is necessary to empty out the old to make room for the new to enter.
Eileen Caddy, Footprints on the Path

Lots of people who want to break habits are so full of all the reasons why they can't change or why it is too difficult that there is hardly any room even to consider an alternative. There is no space in their heads for the idea that changing their habit is possible, even easy. If you are not happy and want to change, the first thing you need to change is your mind. It is your mind, before your body, that can let you down or pick you up.

The Power of Thought

The greatest discovery of my generation is that human beings can alter their lives by altering their attitudes of mind.
William James

I am probably going to surprise you by saying that most people do not know what they want. They know what they *don't* want – for instance their 'bad' habit. But often they do not know what they do want.

If you start programming your body to do something different without first figuring it out in your head, your risk of failure is high. This is why so many people fail to succeed when trying to break a habit. You attract what you focus on, and if when trying to give up you think constantly about food, cigarettes or the feeling of biting your fingernails, that is what you will end up with. Instead of thinking about what we do *not* want, we need to focus on what we *do* want.

Where Is Your Focus?

Many find stopping smoking hard because their focus is on what they are trying to *give up* or *quit* instead of on what they are trying to gain or achieve. The brain gives us what we focus on, so thinking constantly about smoking just makes us want to go on doing it.

'I must do something' will always solve more problems than 'something must be done'.

Consider how you act when trying to achieve or plan another goal in life. When you are booking a holiday, you don't tell the travel agent where you don't want to go. In the supermarket, you do not amble up and down the aisles containing food you've no intention of buying.

Sally, a friend of ours, told us about the time she visited a hairdresser and was impressed when they gave her a form to fill in asking her to detail all the sorts of cuts she disliked and definitely did not want. Having taken about 20 minutes to fill it in, she was confident of leaving with a style suited to her face and lifestyle. But guess what she walked away with? Needless to say, the tears she shed were not those of joy. Left with a long but incomplete list of don'ts, the hairdresser still managed to come up with something Sally hated. It would have been far better if they'd taken the trouble to sound her out on which styles she'd be pleased with.

Good artists, architects, designers and even hairdressers think about and have a vision of what they want to achieve. Rarely do they picture what they do not want to create, or focus on what they do not want – but when they do, as happened in this story, the results can be pretty disastrous.

Now Change Is Possible

Right now, you can change. We have seen people do it. We have watched 60-a-day smokers stop for good. We have seen people lose more weight than they ever dreamed possible. We have seen people become more positive about

In the middle of
difficulty lies
opportunity.
Albert Einstein

themselves and build up their self-esteem, and generally enjoy life more.

We won't give up on you, because we believe in you. We love people who put up their hands and say: 'Hey, I have got a problem and I want to change it,' because what you are saying is you want your life to get better and you are prepared to do something different and new. Now we need you to make that decision to change, and stick with it, whatever it takes. It is often surprising how very little it takes.

Being told by others that stopping smoking (or changing any other habit) is difficult does not mean you will find it difficult. The harsh circumstances some people have to endure, which we cannot even begin to imagine, do not stop them from changing. They simply make a decision, and change.

Pete writes: At the age of five I was told I was dyslexic. Nearly all of my school reports said that I was unable to concentrate, and at the age of 10 a top educational specialist told my parents that I was not an academic child. A-levels and any kind of higher education, they were told, were completely out of the question. I could quite easily have accepted this widely-held view of my academic potential, but I did not. I now have more degrees than GCSEs.

It is not your conditions, but your decisions that will determine whether or not you succeed.

What stage are you at in changing your ways?
Have you made a real decision?
What are the first five things you are going to do differently?
We can help you generate the self-belief, but you must first decide you want it.

Every time we say
'I must do
something' it takes
an incredible
amount of energy.
Far more than
physically doing it.
Gita Bellin

Did you hear about the man who prayed to the goddess asking to win the lottery? 'It shall be done,' came the goddess' reply. When he hadn't won a week later, the man prayed again, begging for a win. 'Yes, all right,' answered the goddess. Another week passed, and still the man had not won. He asked the goddess why. 'For goodness' sake,' she snapped. 'Meet me half-way. Buy a ticket!'

You might think you have bought that winning ticket by buying and now reading this book. But the real ticket to success is doing the exercises and taking the time to change. It is up to you whether you use this ticket. To hit the jackpot, you have to commit yourself.

Start to make the whole process just that bit easier for yourself by thinking of changing your habit not as a problem, but as a challenge. We do understand why you think it is going to be difficult, but this is not the first time we have helped someone break a habit, and you are no different from the many others who have succeeded. We simply showed and taught them how to use their minds to serve them, rather than allow what they have always done to rule their lives.

The simple truth is this: if you carry on doing what you have always done, the chances are you will continue to get the same results. The difference that will make things change is learning how to behave in new ways.

Redirecting Your Attention

An incredible amount of energy goes into continuing with our habits. Procrastinators, those with eating disorders, smokers, etc., are almost always strong people with huge quantities of energy and self-will who are simply misdirecting their potential.

The chains of habit are too weak to be felt until they are too strong to be broken.
Samuel Johnson

Change is never a loss – it is change only.
Vernon Howard,
The Mystic Path
to Cosmic Power

To keep a lamp burning we have to keep putting oil in it.
Mother Teresa

How about your own outdated habit? How much energy and time go into cultivating it? You can change by using that energy and time in more productive ways.

Each of us is responsible for learning whichever behaviour we have – perhaps unintentionally – adopted. If we truly want to change, we must simply apply the same skills we used to acquire the habit to do something more positive.

Some people say they are too lazy to change, but all 'being lazy' means is they don't like the idea of change or believe they can achieve it. People are not lazy when it comes to doing the things they like. It is merely that they associate some form of discomfort with change, and as a result can't motivate themselves to give it a try.

How the Techniques Work

Before we go on, you must know that it is not the techniques themselves which are going to help you to change, but what you *do* with them. Just like developing a habit, it is only through repetition, through practising and applying the techniques, that is going to get results.

We coached a top tennis player in these techniques some time ago, helping him get to the semi-finals of a major tournament. He told us they had worked, but later changed his mind. The techniques stopped working when he stopped practising them.

Generally, you cannot do something once and expect imme-diate results. You would not go into a gym, lift a barbell once

Will today be the day you finally DECIDE that who you are as a person is much more than you've been demonstrating?
Anthony Robbins, Awaken the Giant Within

and expect bigger biceps. You work the muscle by overloading it repeatedly until it responds in a certain way. You push the boundaries of comfort again and again until you get the results you want.

The same goes for this or any other training technique. Repetitive practice makes perfect practice, so do the exercises we give you with conviction, determination and desire, and be committed.

The most damaging phrase in the language is: 'It has always been done that way'.

Attitude

The best professional in any field will do anything they believe will get them to the top; the wannabes won't admit to themselves when something is wrong. So be willing to face and deal with adversity and make mistakes. Each mistake will teach you something, but becoming frustrated and getting cross with yourself for every slip-up will only get you more of what you say you want to change.

You are never really playing against an opponent. You are playing against yourself, your own highest standards And when you reach your limits, that is real joy.
Arthur Ashe

A well-known and very successful footballer told us of how he dealt with a drinking problem: when it got to the point where the drink was interfering in a way he did not like with every aspect of his life, he made a whole-hearted decision to change. Looking back on the experience, he now compares life with the game of football. It does not matter how many times you fall down, because you always will, he says. What matters is what you do when you get back up again.

It is a rough and tough world but there is no substitute for experience, and for experience read experiment. Some succeed, others fail. But failure is not falling down, it is staying down. And that is life on this planet, from The Fall itself. Play to your strengths and the weaknesses fall away.
Robert Harper

Lord, we know what we are, but know not what we may be.
William Shakespeare, Hamlet

For years you might have lived as your parents' you, your friends' you, your teachers' you, your partner's you and your bosses' you, but where on earth are YOU?
Robert Harper

The Champion's Creed

'I am only judged by the number of times I succeed. And the number of times I succeed is in direct proportion to the number of times I can fail and keep trying!'

There is nothing wrong with having habits, and the only thing that is stopping you from moving on is the realization that you can change. You do not have to be this person; you have made yourself into this person, and you are far more than the sum total of your habits.

You are much more than your behaviour, because you can CHANGE your behaviour. Habits might appear to define you – but they don't. You can learn to be different. You might still doubt that you can change, but we are sure you know some-one else in the same or a similar situation to yourself who has broken their habit. You can, too.

The Game We Play

Pete writes: I almost always ask the groups on an eight-week slimming course that I run if there is anything they have always wanted to do but have not yet done. Half-way through one par-ticular course, a woman called Catherine said she used to do a lot of drama, and had been very good at it. Although she had never had the chance to become a professional actress, she was able to use her acting skills to effect change. She began imagining herself behaving in the way she wanted. She saw herself eating more fruit and looking and feeling happier. She wrote down the behaviour she wished to adopt, almost as though she were writing out a new role in a play, then imagined herself playing it. She went on to say

> The greatest pleasure in life is doing what people say you cannot do.
>
> *Walter Bagehot*

that she was changing. 'People had this opinion of me in the office. I used to be the person who, whenever there were chocolate biscuits offered, would have one. I always had sweets and chocolate around me at my desk. Now I don't want that any more. I have a bowl of fruit. People don't like it, they are frightened by it, because I am changing.'

It can sometimes feel strange or even threatening when we change and start to become the person we want to be. It can also be a threat to other people. Catherine was beginning to take on a new way of being which may have felt strange at first, but eventually felt more comfortable and empowering because she was, as last, becoming herself.

The game that most people play is being the same as everyone else. This usually means conforming to a certain way of thinking and being. How do the majority of people think and behave? Generally people focus on what is wrong, what is missing, what they have not got, and give themselves a hard time. They are dissatisfied with their work, often stressed, and have habits that no longer do anything for them.

We are almost relentlessly bombarded with messages that make us focus on what is wrong with and missing from our lives. Television and the media in general tend to reinforce this obsession with problems and unhappy events, presenting us with programmes which have as their highlight disaster, difficulty, death and dysfunctional relationships. Confronted with this, it is hardly surprising so many think for so much of the time about what is wrong, and feel depressed as a result. But think for a moment: is this not just another habit we have learned?

Let's take an example. Do you know any young children who want to be read the front page of a newspaper as a bedtime story? Do they enjoy watching the news? No. They like to watch and listen to stories with happy endings. They like to laugh. On average, children laugh and smile about 400 times a day, according to a recent study. By the time they are adults, this figure has dropped to 15 times a day. Is it important to laugh and smile? Yes, because each time you do so, natural drugs (endorphins) are released in the body which make you feel good. Try it now:

Smile three times.

You should feel the difference almost immediately.

One of the biggest habits people have is 'terminal serious-ness' – they take themselves too seriously. So, for the next couple of days, see how many times you laugh or even smile. You could well be shocked by the result.

Is the game that everyone else plays the one you want to go on playing? Or do you want to start playing the game of your own life, doing the things that feel right and that you want to do, and not those you think you should be doing?

Start to make up your own rules.
What do you really want?
Do you want to get rid of this habit you have?
Then do it!
You do not have to believe any longer that you can't.

When young, elephants that are trained for the circus are attached to a stake in the ground by a heavy chain. As much as they try to

The mind is the limit. As long as the mind can envision the fact that you can do something, you can do it, as long as you believe 100 per cent.
Arnold Schwarzenegger

To change one's life: start immediately. Do it flamboyantly. No exceptions, no excuses.
William James

It's lack of faith that makes people afraid of meeting challenges, and I believed in myself.
Muhammad Ali

pull away, they cannot, until one day they give up trying. From then on they can be chained up with nothing more than a rope. Whenever these elephants later experiences any degree of resistance, they give up trying to fight it. They are conditioned to believe it is impossible to pull away, and their behaviour follows their belief.

You have been told you cannot give up your habit. You might have believed for a long time that you cannot give up the habit. You have felt as though a heavy chain has attached you to the belief and you've stopped trying to pull away. Try on the idea of being tied to your habit with thread: see how easy it is to break?

Committing Yourself to Change

What precedes all behaviours, actions and performances? What turns a dream into a reality? The answer is *decisions*. Your decisions determine what you think, how you feel, what you do and whom you become.

It is often your decisions, and not your conditions, that hold you back. If you make the decision and choose to make some different choices to the ones you are making now, you will succeed.

How come some people can break their habits while others can't? It is because they make different decisions. They commit to achieving, and do whatever it takes to succeed.

Do you know it is estimated that about 90 per cent of people who buy books do not read past the first chapter?

The easiest thing for you to do now is not read any more. If you do decide to read on, you could just as easily read it half-heartedly and skip over all the exercises. That is how most people read books like this.

The simple fact is that the more you put into this book, the more you will get out of it.

That is why we want you not only to make a real decision to change, but also to make a contract with yourself. Don't worry, it is not legally binding – but it will help to get you focused and committed to breaking your habit. It is your actions, remember, that will generate success.

Make a firm commitment to break your habit, because this commitment will unlock the energy to achieve it.

Contract

I will do the exercises in this book regularly and with determination, and add to my daily life those that work best for me.
I will honour my decision to break my habit and become a happier and healthier person.
I can and will succeed.

Signed: _____

Dated: _____

step 2

Using Your Imagination

There is little
sense in
attempting to
change external
conditions, you
must first change
your inner beliefs,
then outer
conditions will
change
accordingly.

Brian Adams,
How to Succeed

Now that we are ready to start the exercises, you must understand that not all of them will necessarily work for everyone. Some will prove more effective than others, but you need to do them all. If you don't, how will you ever know which ones really work for you?

As we've already said, so many people who buy self-help books only do the exercises half-heartedly, or read through them and think: 'I will come back to these later.' We challenge you to give the exercises that follow all the effort you can, and embrace the changes that you are going to make.

Most of us are familiar with that old adage: Nothing beats experience. This expression applies to these exercises as much as to anything else. The 5th-century BC philosopher Lao-Tse wrote: 'If you tell me, I will listen. If you show me, I will see. But if you let me experience, I will learn.'

The first time you do an exercise, you might think: 'That was interesting,' and be tempted not to do it again. It is the

Take rest; a field
that has rested
gives a beautiful
crop.

Ovid

All good work is
done the way ants
do things, little by
little.

Lafcadio Hearn

accumulative effect of repeating these exercises over and over, almost to the point of monotony, that gets results. You must have been over them so many times that when you come to repeat an exercise for the umpteenth time you want to say: 'Oh yes, but I *know*.' And hopefully by then you *will*, because you will have convinced your brain that this is how you want to behave.

We do not want you to do one exercise straight after another. There is no rush. If you want to make progress, each of the exercises needs to be done a number of times over a few days or weeks before you move on to the next one, with appropriate rests in between.

It has been discovered in tests that performance is far superior when there are spaces or gaps between practice sessions. When spaces of time are not left, it has been found, the learner's performance improves, but reaches a plateau. If breaks are allowed, however, performance tends to exceed the level previously reached.

As well as encouraging you to take breaks, we have also inserted between some of the main exercises smaller, occasionally more physical exercises to add a bit more fun to the process and also to break up what can be a fairly intense experience.

⊘ Whenever you do any of the exercises, try to ensure you are as free as possible from distractions.
⊘ Always have a notebook and pen handy.
⊘ When preparing to do an exercise, remember that if you want things to look up, you will have start doing so. Your head must be up and your eyes on the horizon when beginning an exercise, because when you look down you start talking negatively to yourself.

The thinking that got you into this is not going to be the thinking that gets you out of it.

Michael Breen

Exercise

1 Stop for a moment now and look up.
2 Smile.
3 While you are smiling, try to feel depressed.

When we *feel* down, guess what? We tend to *look* down. When we feel good, our eyes tend to look straight ahead or above.

Choose Your Words Carefully

Many of the people we help to give up habits talk about having two sides to themselves: one which wants them to give up, and another which is able to persuade them to carry on. One woman came to see us because she thought she ought to give up smoking. She described the part of her that wished to give up as being her angelic and pure side who knew it would be better for her health, while the darker, more rebellious side wanted to keep her hooked on cigarettes, reasoning that she still enjoyed smoking and should not be dictated to by others. We find this scenario fairly typical among those who wish to give up a habit. They feel they *should* or *ought* to, and do not necessarily – to begin with, at least – actually *want* to. We asked this woman to tell us how she felt when she said: 'I should give up.' 'Completely demotivated,' was her reply.

People do not realize that the words they use about their intention can radically affect how they feel about giving up a habit. How many of us do the things we *should* do, and how many the things we *want* to?

Think about your own habit and say to yourself, for example: 'I should stop biting my nails.' Notice how it feels when you say this.

Now repeat this sentence, using each of the words in the list below. Notice which one makes you feel most motivated to change. We are not asking you to find which words make you *believe* you can change, just which feel best for you.

We challenge you, with the words you choose, to say this personalized sentence over and over to yourself, like you really mean it, whether or not you believe it right now.

I should	I have
I must	I can
I will	I hope to
I am going to	I may
I aim to	I am
I could	I might

Now, when you say this to yourself ('I can be healthy,' 'I will be slim,' 'I have high self-confidence,' 'I want to be in control'), what do you picture? Think about what you want to achieve, not what you want to leave behind. See yourself as being there already.

The words you choose must, when you say them to yourself, make you feel as though you are actually going to live them. If they don't, it is unlikely they will be of much help, because changing a habit is all about changing your feelings towards it, and yourself.

Can you imagine how you would look and feel once your habit is broken? Where in your body does that feeling start? Can you imagine that feeling being twice as strong? Start practising feeling like that *now*.

Pete writes: I once worked with an agoraphobic, someone who has a phobia about going out and being around people. She rang me in desperation, having tried many different therapies, and asked if I could come to her house. When I told her she would have to come to see me she protested, saying she had not left her house for more than two years. I said the best I could do was meet her half-way. After thinking about it for 10 minutes she rang back suggesting we meet at a hotel two miles from where she lived. I agreed immediately, knowing that in being willing to travel just a short distance from home, she was serious about changing. I met her at the hotel and, within an hour of doing a few exercises, some of which are included in this book, we were in a bar having a drink, had gone to a supermarket, and done many other outdoor things she had not done for a very long time. This woman really had stepped outside of her comfort zone. Yet I knew that once I was gone the easiest thing for her would have been to go back to doing what she had done before. In order to overcome her phobia properly she needed constantly to push the boundaries of what was comfortable. I asked her to make a contract with herself to honour this and her decision to change.

Have you made a decision yet, or are you still sceptical? Are you going to honour your decision to change?

> However many holy words you read, however many you speak, what good will they do you if you do not act upon them?
> *The Dhammapada*

> All you have to do to change your life is to change your mind. It really is that simple, but it isn't always easy. All you have to do to stop feeling bad is to start feeling good ... but feeling good is not a one-time event; it is a decision we make minute-by-minute, day by day. It is a creation.

> He who has begun his task has half done it.
> *Horace*

Imagination is
more important
than knowledge.
    Albert Einstein

The Power of the Imagination

Many people actually have no idea how the brain works. It is an amazing piece of equipment and, although it has powers and capabilities that science has not yet discovered, there is still plenty we know.

One of the problems is that no one ever gets a manual telling them how to get the best from their brain. There is no way of finding out how to break unwanted habits or how to feel great all the time or how to build supreme confidence.

Pete writes: As I child I could not spell properly. Until I was 21 I used to try to write every single word phonetically, because that was the only way I had been taught how. Then I met someone who showed me how to visualize words, a technique used by many good spellers. I tried it, and from then on could spell. It was simply a matter of learning a new and very easy way of how to do some-thing differently.

In much the same way we want to help you to develop your own 'user manual' which will allow you to break any unwanted habits and live the life you want to lead. In helping you to develop that manual, this book provides many powerful strategies and techniques that have already helped thou-sands of people to break their habits.

We've already mentioned the importance of making a decision, because it is your decision that unlocks the action necessary to break a habit. The main tool that is going to help you is learning how to use your mind in more powerful and productive ways. And the first step in doing this is learn-ing how to use your imagination.

Everyone uses their imagination all the time, but not necessarily in particularly effective or productive ways.

If I were to ask you:

⊘ What did you have for dinner last night?
⊘ Where was your last holiday?
⊘ What colour is an orange?
⊘ What does your best friend look like?

You'd immediately make a picture of them.

Using your imagination in this way is also known as 'visualization'. We prefer to call it *effective thinking*. Visualization is not a technique – as we have shown, you already do it every day. It is how human beings process information about their world. The difference is how you *use* this inbuilt skill.

Some people are naturally more visual than others, but we can all learn to visualize effectively. We once worked with the English Blind Cricket Team and even they, when playing, would make visual representations of where the ball was and where they were running. Visualization only becomes a technique when we put it to particular use.

In one research experiment three groups of basketball players were prepared for practice. The first group was allowed on to the court to practise with a ball, the second group was allowed on to the court but were told just to imagine themselves playing there, while the third group was left in a room to imagine themselves playing. Each group was told to try to get the ball into the basket as many times as possible. Once each group had had time to practise in their respective ways, all were allowed on to the court to see which would score the most points. The first group were

Dreams come
true: without that
possibility, nature
would not incite us
to have them.
John Updike

not very much improved over their normal performance, as they'd in effect been practising missing as well as scoring. The second group had improved but, being on the court, had also imagined themselves missing. It was the third group, all of whom, in the seclusion of a room away from the court, had imagined themselves scoring every time, which got the ball through the hoop most often.

The things we think about and imagine have a profound effect on how we feel. Thinking about or imagining how you will be once your habit is broken gives your brain a description of where you want it to take you. Doing this should also make you feel good, and because making you feel good is one of the brain's primary functions, the thought or imagining becomes a way of behaving that the brain wishes to adopt.

When you commit yourself mentally to changing a habit, and start practising having made that change, the change will happen. You could just as easily decide not to, but those who really want to change will work at it repeatedly until they get the desired result.

So, visualization is no more than a tool many of us already use, but are perhaps unaware of doing so. When you are reading a good book or remembering a particular event in the past, you are more often than not using mental pictures to be able to recall the story. As a child you probably imagined vividly and often acted out how you wished to be as an adult. In any of these instances you are using visualization.

Some people say they have trouble using their imagination in this way. A little practice is always useful, as we will be using visualization quite a lot in the exercises that follow:

1 Picture the front door of your home.

2 What colour is it?

3 Imagine you have painted it another colour.

4 Now that you can see it clearly, give the door horizontal stripes in another colour.

5 Now make the stripes vertical.

6 Change the shape of the door knob and, then give the door a letter box.

7 See a cat walking through the cat flap at the bottom and notice what the door mat looks like.

8 Now imagine moving the door closer to you, then pushing it away.

9 Move it to the left and then to the right.

10 Now open it, and imagine walking into your home.

11 What kind of flooring do you have?

12 Are there any pets roaming around?

Visualization is just a fancy word for remembering what something looked like, or imagining what something might look like. You have been doing it all day, every day, all your life.

1 Picture an orange.

2 See the orange getting bigger and bigger and bigger until it is the size of a football.

3 Now imagine the orange turns purple, and yellow spots appear all over it.

4 The spots light up and start flashing like the coloured lights at a disco.

5 Now imagine the spots disappear, and in their place is a cheeky, smiley face.

6 The face starts laughing and you can see two rows of beautiful pearly white teeth.

7 Imagine the orange laughing so hard that tears start squirting from the eyes.

8 The orange stops laughing now, and slowly the face disappears.

9 The orange starts to shrink until it is the size of a ping-pong ball.

10 Imagine that it starts bouncing up and down, higher and higher, until the force of the impact on the ground makes it break.

11 Splattered orange lies all over the floor.

12 Now the bits start to shrivel and shrink until they vanish.

1 See a picture of yourself feeling confident on a television screen.

2 Notice the look on your face and what you are wearing.

3 The screen gets bigger and bigger and moves towards you until you can step into it.

4 Now step into it.

5 How does it feel to wear the clothes of the confident you?

6 How does it feel to be in that state of mind?

7 Register and remember that feeling.

After trying these exercises, some people still struggle to visualize. I then get them to imagine being on a rollercoaster or, if they have a fear of heights, watching others enjoy the ride. If in using your imagination in this way you can incorporate all of your senses, it should give you a full sensory experience.

The soul never thinks without a picture.

Aristotle

1 Imagine sitting on (or watching) a rollercoaster.

2 You are sitting right at the front and the carriages are full.

3 The metal safety bar comes down in front of you.

4 You grip it. The metal is cold.

5 Loud music is pumping all around you, like at a fairground.

6 With a jolt, the ride begins.

7 Slowly you begin to climb the first incline.

8 You cannot see what is over the top, but below you, to your left and to your right, the crowds are getting smaller.

9 As you get higher, the noise of the crowd gets quieter and seems to echo in the air.

10 Your adrenaline is rising and your grip on the safety bar tightens.

11 Your carriage reaches the top of the first peak, and with a big WHOOOOOSH it descends at great speed.

12 You can feel the wind against your face and the pressure on your body as it is pressed back into the seat.

13 You let out a big 'YEEHAAAAAOOOOOOOOOOOOH!'

14 The ride slows at the bottom, but immediately picks up speed again as you face the loop-the-loop.

15 There is no time even to think.

16 Next you know you are upside down, trying to force your head back on the seat as the speed of the ride forces it forwards.

17 Your stomach feels as though it has been turned inside-out as the ride slows down.

18 You get off, legs a little wobbly, exhilarated and a little relieved that it is over.

To find yourself,
think for yourself.
Socrates

From now on, become more aware of how you use your mind to visualize. When you are reading or when someone is telling you a story, think about the pictures you automatically conjure up in your head. At some point in the next hour, or as soon as you are able to, go and find a children's book, preferably one without pictures, and just read a couple of pages. Be aware of the pictures you make in your mind.

Getting into the Right State for Change

Pete writes: From Monday to Friday I used to spend most of my time being just slightly anxious. Since becoming aware of that, I have really slowed down. I still have as much to do and as many things to worry about, but the anxiety was not helping. Only through being more relaxed and objective was I able to become aware of and change what I was doing.

Think of an average day in your life in terms of a 24-hour clock. There is a good chance you spend at least eight of those hours asleep, relaxed, but what about the rest? How much of that time do you spend angry, stressed, worried, upset, and how much relaxed, smiling or laughing?

Grab your notebook. Now, if you are ready to start thinking for yourself, write down, as you hear it, the constant chatter that goes on in your head. It never ceases to amaze us how much self-defeating nonsense comes out. Take a break, switch off and try it now.

On another day, try being a 'state manager' – make a note of *what* you feel, and *when*.

For now, think about the sort of state you would like to spend most of your time in. Describe it here:

Being happy, sad, depressed, anxious or surprised are all states that people experience, but there is a state that is much more spontaneous and free, observant yet without judgement, relaxed and aware, comfortable. Just being.

There is a very important and particular state to be in if we want to make change. Reading or doing any of the exercises we give you when you are angry or stressed will probably be counterproductive. You need to be in a relaxed and resourceful state when turning to this book.

Tho Habit-busting State

Have you ever noticed that when you feel relaxed, confident and happy, you also feel in control? This is the most effective state to be in when trying to break a habit. By way of finding out what 'being in control' means to different people, we ask them to imagine what they would look like when 'in control'.

⊘ What is your breathing like?
⊘ What is the look in your eyes?
⊘ See that picture of yourself on a screen. When it is clear, move it closer to you.

⊘ As the picture gets bigger and closer, it moves into you
   and becomes you.
⊘ How does it feel to be that person?
⊘ Now imagine seeing yourself 10 times more relaxed and
   in control.
⊘ See it on a movie screen in brilliant colour with surround
   sound.
⊘ Amplify that image another 20 times, and move the
   picture closer until you are that picture.
⊘ Now, say whatever it is you want, for example: 'I want to
   be slimmer,' 'I want to be on time,' 'I want to be
   successful.'

Because the brain is like a muscle, it needs to warmed up
before it starts to work. To make the exercises designed to
help you break your habit more effective, you must first do
this quick and simple exercise to get your brain warmed up
and ready.

The technique will help you to feel relaxed yet in control,
and will get you in the right state or frame of mind for
change. An icon representing this warm-up exercise (*) will
appear before most other exercises, to remind you to do this
one first. (It is also a technique you could use to get you in
the right state for an important event, such as a public
speech, job interview or exam.)

Exercise to Get You into the Right State for Change *

Getting into the right state for change usually means feeling relaxed and in control. Other words used by those we

have worked with to describe themselves in a positive and productive state and ready for change are: calm, expectant, interested, alert, ready to go, excited. Think of a word or phrase that describes the state in which you know you can achieve.

1 With your eyes closed or open, imagine a picture of yourself in a state that could be described by using any of the words mentioned before, including any of your own.

2 See that picture in front of you and notice how far away it is.

3 Now imagine it moving towards you, getting bigger the closer it gets, until the picture moves inside you, so you become the picture and take on the feeling of being more calm, or expectant, interested or alert, ready to go, excited, etc.

4 You are in control and relaxed.

5 Now, imagine another picture of yourself, looking much the same as the last, except now you are looking five times more in control and relaxed, interested or alert.

6 The picture is brighter, more colourful and more real.

7 It moves closer to you and now moves inside you around your heart area.

8 You can feel, from the top of your head down to your toes, that much more relaxed and in control.

9 Now make another picture, even better than the last – you are twice again as relaxed and in control.

10 The picture has a volume and clarity that surpasses anything in the two pictures you imagined before.

11 It moves closer to you, inside you and around your heart, which is pumping the feeling all around your body with every breath. This feeling of excitement, control and being relaxed is flowing with the blood in your veins.

Do this exercise again and again until you are ready, with that relaxed and controlled feeling, to do your first real habit-breaking technique (the first one appears on page 98).

(You could also use this exercise when you are in a stressful situation and you know people will tempt you to lose control.)

The Pen Trick

Put a pen in your mouth so that both ends of your mouth stick out and it forces you to smile. The position of the pen should keep your face in a smiling expression. Your mind and body will begin to produce neurotransmitters which cause you to feel good because these neural pathways are helping to build a new vision of what you believe you are and what you can achieve (as discussed in Step One). You will, by repeatedly seeing a 'new you' in your mind's eye, reinforce those pathways in your brain telling you that you feel good. Make that feeling the start of feeling good just because you can!

Getting Results

In putting these steps to work we need to add in the emotional and mental responses we attach to certain experiences. For when we see or visualize what we want, it is not merely in picture form, but should actually be a full sensory experience. Use your imagination dramatically – you must be able to feel, hear, smell and taste as well as see the new you. It must be as if you are there.

Here's another preparatory exercise to try:

1   Sit comfortably, free from distraction, keeping your eyes open or closed, whichever suits you.
2   Remember the best holiday you have ever had.
3   Recall some of the things you saw or heard on this holiday, the things you smelled and tasted, and some of the things you felt.
4   Imagine being back on that holiday now.
5   Make it more real and more colourful even than you remember it.
6   Now take a couple of deep breaths. Feeling good, slowly open your eyes.
7   Take a short break, then close your eyes again (if you wish).
8   Now imagine being on a make-believe holiday.
9   Imagine you are on a beautiful beach with white sand and clear blue water.
10 You can hear the gentle sound of the waves and the seagulls calling out high in the sky.
11 You can smell the sea air and almost taste the salt.
12 You feel warm, peaceful and relaxed.
13 Take a deep breath and open your eyes.

Although you know the difference, your brain cannot distinguish between the real and the imagined holiday. The more you think about the one you made up, the more your brain starts to think that it is real. Because the nervous system cannot distinguish between a real and an imagined experience, if practised enough, the thoughts we have become a plan of what we are going to do. And the more clearly thought-out and distinctive our desire, the more passionately we will pursue it. One of the keys to breaking a habit is to start imagining your life in the future, free from the habit, doing things differently and being in control. You get what you focus on.

Think About What You Want

Instead of thinking about what they would *like* to happen, most people think about what they do *not* want to happen by picturing things going wrong.

You say you want to change, and have read this far. Maybe you do want change. Are you ready to use your imagination now you know that it is possible? Write down what you want to achieve.

I want _____

_____

If in the space above you have written 'to stop smoking', 'to stop procrastinating' or 'to stop being stressed', what immediately comes to mind? In order not to think about something, you need first to think of it. The effect of this is to leave you focused on what you don't want, which is why you have probably found stopping in the past so difficult. The picture that comes to mind as you write out your description is of you doing whichever habit it is you want to break. You need to use a different approach.

Write down in the slot 'to be in control', 'to be on time' or 'to be more positive' instead. You will be creating a representation of something that you want your brain to find more evidence to support. This is what really can set you free from your habit.

If one desires a change, one must be that change before that change can take place.
Gita Bellin

⊘ We all like the idea of being in control.

⊘ What is the picture you can see of yourself in control?

⊘ Can you see it well enough to describe it in detail?

⊘ Look at what you are wearing, the expression on your face, feel what 'in control' means to you.

⊘ Now step inside the picture.

⊘ Make the feeling of being the you that is in control twice as strong.

⊘ How do you feel about breaking your habit now?

The New You

If you want to give up something, you need to be able to see yourself how you want to be. In other words, you need to be able to see yourself as already having given up whatever habit it is you no longer wish to have. You need to pretend, to imagine how you would be living your life as a non-smoker or former procrastinator, and how you might like to react in different sets of circumstances. The more you can use your imagination to help you in this, the more successful you are likely to be, because by imagining yourself as vividly as possible as this ex-habit person, you are allowing your body to prepare for the end result.

Exercise

⊘ Think of the you without the habit.
⊘ What would the world look like through their eyes?
⊘ What would it be like to wear their clothes?
⊘ How would they stand, walk or sit?
⊘ How would they say 'no', and mean it?

To begin to see your own potential, try this (you may need someone to read this to you, or you could tape-record it):

1 Stand up with your feet shoulder-width apart and point with whichever hand you write straight out in front of you.

2 Now, without moving your feet, rotate in the direction of your extended arm as far as you can go. You are now probably pointing towards something behind you. Make a mental note of where you are pointing.

3 Twist back and, with both arms at your sides, close your eyes and imagine yourself with your arm extended very slowly rotating round to the point you reached before, and then a bit further.

4 Imagine doing this again, very slowly, and then again.

5 Now imagine it again, this time with a bright colour coming out through your body and extending down your arm.

6 Imagine this again – this time you can reach even further, possibly all the way round.

7 Keeping your eyes closed, lift your arm up and imagine reaching round again, and again, and again so you picture yourself going all the way round several times without stopping.

Right now take one step (even if it's a small micro-movement) in the direction of your dreams.

8 Open your eyes and, at the same speed, start to move your arm round. If you can, get a friend to gently push your arm as far as it will physically go.

9 You should find you can pivot several inches further than when you tried the first time. No warm-up, no flexibility exercise. Just the power of the mind.

What do you think this exercise demonstrates? That really you have no idea just how capable you are, if you can just get over the limitations your brain inadvertently puts on you. The time has come for you to realize that you have more potential than you ever thought.

Are Your Focus and Decision in Sync?

Pete writes: Years ago, when I was teaching a lot of aerobics and playing lots of sport, I had a groin injury which was very painful. Nothing I tried would help or cure it. Never having tried alternative medicine before, I nevertheless in desperation went to see an acupuncturist. He sat me down and said, 'What do you want?' I replied, 'Well, I have got this pain and it really hurts.' He then said, 'What are you actually here for?' I said, 'Well, I can't play football and I can't teach aerobics and it is really sore and is upsetting me.' He then stopped me and said, 'Look, if you can't tell me what you want, there is the door – use it.' I suddenly thought, 'What do I want?', and realized I had not even thought about it. I knew what I *didn't* want, and that is what I had been focused on. Eventually I said: 'I just want back that comfortable freedom of movement that I used to have.' He said: 'Right, lie down.' I focused on what I

Nothing is so
exhausting as
indecision, and
nothing so futile.
Bertrand Russell

wanted and, after having carried the injury for two years, the pain was gone in just six sessions.

How much of the cure was down to the acupuncture and how much due to switching my focus, I don't know, but what I do know is that as soon as I started to think about what I wanted, I experienced change.

When asked what they want, almost invariably people talk about what they do not want. We see this pattern repeated again and again.

Pete: 'Hello there. Well, you have come here to see me today; can you tell me what you want?'

Client: 'Well, I am feeling really bad. I just split up with my boyfriend.'

Pete: 'I'm sorry. But can you tell me what you want?'

Client: 'Well, you see, a while ago I went out with this person who was really horrible, seeing other people while supposedly dating me, and I found out about it.'

Pete: 'Mmm, OK. Can you tell me why you are actually here?'

Client: 'Well, you know, I am here because I just can't seem to attract the right partner.'

Pete: 'Well yes, OK, but what is it that you actually want?'

Client: 'Well, nobody loves me.'

See what we mean?

Once you have made a decision to change, focus on that, and not on what you are leaving behind. Remember that it is your *decision*, not your *condition*, that is going to determine whether you go forward or back.

Things do not
change: we
change.

*Henry David
Thoreau*

Staying Focused on What You Want

During a very important golf tournament some years ago the professional golfer Arnold Palmer was about to take a shot when a train passed loudly and his ball went into the rough. Afterwards his caddy said to Palmer: 'It was a shame about that train, wasn't it, coming past just as you were going to play that ball,' to which Palmer replied: 'What train?'

So deeply focused had he been on the shot, Palmer had completely shut himself off from everything else. Anyone can do this. We must just find what we need and delete what is not necessary or what is not working, instead of becoming uptight and often preoccupied by it.

Remember that at any time your behaviour is optional. You may well, at times, feel compelled to act or react to situations in certain ways, but that is just practice. You can choose whether to moan to yourself over having lapsed from your intention to break a habit, or you can laugh about it and move on. Always, it is up to you.

- ⊘ Where is your focus now?
- ⊘ Take a deep breath and go to the part of your body that fecls the best.
- ⊘ Have you found it?
- ⊘ There is every chance that in doing so you went first to the part that felt worst. You are not the first person to have done this, and you certainly won't be the last. Focus is determined by practice.

Perseverance furthers.
I Ching, Chinese Book of Changes

If you do not live it, you do not believe it.

⊘ Can you remember an event with particular significance or one that stands out in your mind that occurred in the last six months?

⊘ Was it good or bad?

⊘ Often events that stick with us are bad ones, and that is what more generally we tend to focus on.

⊘ Concentrate on what is right and what you want to make right, and that eventually is what you will get.

In order to set change in motion, we need to discard and rebuild some of our own beliefs about ourselves. As we do this, those around us will start to see and react to the new person we believe we can be. We can choose to believe that there is really not a lot of comfort in so-called comfort eating, but instead a great deal of discomfort. We could start calling it 'discomfort eating' and associate being cheered up with something else, an aromatherapy bath perhaps. You might feel as though you are fooling yourself first time round, but it is simply a matter of establishing a new habit to replace the old. You can do any number of things to take your mind off those cigarettes or chocolate biscuits, and actually get good at whatever you do instead.

Your behaviour does not have to control your life. You have the resources and the ability to change. By learning to take control over pleasure and pain and making new choices about what you associate pleasure and pain with, you can alter your focus, renew your behaviour and change your life.

Future You

Pete writes: I was sitting in a sauna one day listening to a man telling his friend how impossible he found trying to give up smoking. After about 10 minutes of listening to his complaining I stopped him and asked if he could imagine himself in the future, in all the particular instances during which he smokes, not smoking. He said no. This was why he was finding it so difficult to stop.

If you want to change, you must be able to see yourself having made that change or you will have little chance of ever achieving it.

1 Get into state*
2 Stand up and imagine that your front door is before you, life-size, and behind the door is the future you without the habit.
3 The door opens and you can see the back of yourself, in the future, having broken the habit.
4 Notice the difference in what you are wearing and how you feel.
5 Now the you in the future is going to turn to the side so you can see them in profile.
6 Then they move to face you. They look vibrant, amazing and full of life.
7 See the future you as clearly as you like. Move them around so you can get a really good look.
8 Now imagine stepping into the future you and feeling how it is to have broken the habit.
9 Now do it again; step into the future you and intensify that feeling.

You control your future, your destiny. What you think about comes about. By recording your dreams and goals on paper, you set in motion the process of becoming the person you most want to be. Put your future in good hands – your own.
March Victor Hansen

10 Feel the change in every cell of your body, your organs and your bones.

11 Now, physically take a step forward, into the future you.

12 Feel how it feels, see through those eyes and hear through those ears, life without the habit.

13 Once you have finished, take a few deep breaths and have a break.

When you are ready do the exercise again, this time imagine you've been practising it for years. *Practise this exercise every day.*

A mission could be defined as an image of a desired state that you want to get to. Once fully seen, it will inspire you to act, fuel your motivation and determine your behaviour.
Charles Garfield

Goal-Setting – Getting What You Want

What is goal-setting? We believe it is getting what you want. As should be clear by now, your brain can only follow the instructions you give it. To over-ride your habit, you need to give the brain a new set of well thought-out and quite specific instructions, over and over again. The instructions, or new goal(s), need to be so attractive that your brain wants to leave behind your habits and move towards the new you.

In order to get what you want, you need to KNOW what you want. How often do you hear people say: 'It would be nice to have a widget, but I don't know, I am just not sure if that is what I really want.' Is it any wonder most people don't achieve their goals? You must be as clear as you can be about what it is you want to achieve.

Do you have a clear idea of your own direction?

> You've got to think about 'big things' while you are doing small things, so that the small things go in the right direction.
>
> *Alvin Toffler*

 Exercise

Get your notebook.

*Get into state.

1 Have your list of what you want to achieve in front of you. Is it specific and positive enough? For example, 'I want to be slimmer'/'I want to be boss of my company'/'I want to exude confidence.' Negative goals give you only what you do *not* want.

2 When you think about achieving your goal, can you experience it in every sense? Do you know how it will smell, taste, sound and look as well as feel? Think about that now. How do you feel about it? Unless you feel extremely good in every sense when thinking about what you want, it is unlikely you will spend much time on it.

3 How much control do you have? The more people who need to be influenced by way of getting what you want, the harder it is going to be to achieve. But this does not mean you cannot achieve it.

4 Do you have a plan? We can only climb mountains one step at a time. Think about the steps you will need to take in order to get closer to what you want. In order to make getting started easier and to help improve your motivation, break down your desired achievement into a series of mini-achievements. This will allow you to track and celebrate your progress as you move towards what you want, and give you the opportunity to make amendments or correct mistakes along the way.

5 Does it fit in with the rest of your life? If it doesn't, that will have to change too.

Circumstances may cause interruptions and delay, but never lose sight of your goal. Prepare yourself in every way you can by increasing your knowledge and adding to your experience, so that you can make the most of opportunity when it occurs.

Mario Andretti, racing car driver

Once you are satisfied with the checklist above, think again about what you want. Write it down, say it out loud to yourself, picture yourself as already having achieved it. Then, sitting somewhere comfortably, with ample time at your disposal and perhaps playing your favourite music, answer the following questions:

1 What do I want, specifically?

2 When, where and with whom do I want it?

3 What will be different as a result of achieving this?

4 How will I know when I have got it?

5 What will achieving this do for me, get for me or give me?

6 How do I feel about it?

7 What resources do I need to achieve it?

8 What will I see, hear, feel, smell and taste once I have achieved it?

9 How will I look and sound once I have achieved it?

10 What will happen if I achieve this?

11 What won't happen if I achieve this?

12 What will happen if I don't achieve this?

13 What won't happen if I don't achieve this?

14 What would I be able to keep by not achieving this?

15 How do I know that what I want is worth having?

16 How will having it affect my life, my family, my job, my friends?

The answers will give you an idea of what needs to happen if you want to achieve what you want.

step 3

Why We Want to Change: Pleasure vs Pain

Learning to Be Different ...

At any moment I could start being a better person – but which moment should I choose?
Ashleigh Brilliant

Some people who want to break a habit are motivated to change out of disgust and discomfort with themselves and their habit. The discomfort of smoking, eating or drinking too much, for example, is so huge that they can take no more and want to move as far away from it as possible. Others who want to break habits want to look and feel different; they are motivated to move towards something better.

Because the brain tries to steer us clear of any sort of pain, once we begin to experience discomfort because of a habit, the desire to change can be born. Over-riding the brain's old instruction to continue with the habit is all that seems to make change hard.

We might want to stop smoking so we can breathe more clearly, or eat fewer biscuits so we can look and be slimmer, but because these habits have felt so much a part of us they can also appear impossible to break, even when we want to.

He that will not
apply new
remedies must
expect new evils.
Francis Bacon

But if we do not break them, the results of the behaviour can only get worse.

You cannot lose weight if you continue to eat half a packet of biscuits at tea time; you cannot wake up in the morning without a chesty cough if you don't first give up smoking; you cannot have long fingernails to file and paint unless you learn to stop biting them; and you can never be happy if you continuously give yourself a hard time. Change cannot happen, either, if you keep moaning about how difficult it is.

... By Changing Our Thinking Habits

Reproduction and survival are most often cited as the two driving forces of human life. We are not so sure. Why are you reading this book? We believe it is because what drives people in life is their desire to feel good.

One of the major functions of the brain is to avoid pain and make us feel good, but we know from experience that what the brain *believes* is best and what we *know* is best are not always the same.

How many of the people you know feel good about themselves? Probably not many. It is likely that most will behave in ways they think will make them feel better. In other words, they have habits. Regardless of whether the habits work, the majority will keep hold of them.

Pleasure and Pain

One cannot get through life without pain ...
What we can do is choose how to use the pain life presents to us.
Bernie S. Siegel

It is not actual pain that drives us, but our fear that something will lead to pain. And it's not actual pleasure that drives us, but our belief – our sense of certainty – that somehow taking a certain action will lead to pleasure. We're not driven by the reality, but by our perception of reality.
Anthony Robbins,
Awaken the Giant
Within

What do you think motivates most people? It is not so much the anticipated pleasure of changing that motivates many of us at first to want to kick a habit, but the amount of physical, mental or emotional pain we eventually find ourselves in.

In most cases the addict does not want to give up because they suddenly remember how life was before, but because they are so sick of who they have become. The overweight person does not want to start shedding pounds in anticipation of how they will look in a bikini or swim-suit come summer, but because they are sick of how they look and feel.

But where each can come unstuck in their attempt to change is in failing to think *beyond* the consequences of their current behaviour. The addict who has been clean for a time meets a friend who invites him to take some drugs, or the overweight person, now dieting, is offered a cream bun. Both of them make pictures of the immediate after-effects of indulging their habit, decide these effects will not be so dire, and then indulge.

People can, however, learn to think about what is beyond the immediate picture, idea or impression. If either of these two cases had thought about the longer-term repercussions of continuing with their behaviour – starting the drug habit again, the coming down from the high, the robbing to feed the habit, the loss of friends, the eventual destitution; in the case of the overweight person, the guilt after having eaten the cream bun, the feeling of bloatedness, the further weight gained from continuing to eat them – the chances are that, if each of these people had really thought the consequences through, they wouldn't have given in to the immediate temptation.

Persistence takes practice. You know what it takes to convince yourself not to give in. Imagine a situation where you could have indulged your habit, and didn't. Mentally rehearse not giving in to your habit in different circumstances, until that is the way you are.

We worked once with an overweight woman who had started to slim down by being careful about what she ate – until somebody said something that upset her. Out came the sugary foods, which she once again started to eat. Once she was back with us we got her to practise thinking beyond the momentary delight she experienced biting into a piece of chocolate cake to what her reflection in the mirror might look like in six months' time if she continued to eat in that way. She would undoubtedly be fatter, perhaps too fat even to sit in her favourite chair, and probably find herself breathless when trying to climb the stairs. Even getting out of bed could become difficult. The more she thought about this, the greater her motivation to change.

Wake Up to Your Thoughts and Where They Are Leading You

Being aware of how we think about our habits helps us to change them. By substituting the thought of the immediate pleasure we gain from them with the longer-term pain this will mean, we can start wanting to stop.

A woman we worked with said that for years she had the same depressing thoughts every morning when travelling on the bus to work. When she'd first started taking that journey to work she was going through a particularly tough time in her life, but the depressing thoughts did not stop, even once the situation passed. Because she had learned that behaviour when travelling to work, the association remained, and so did the thoughts.

This is known by some as *anchoring* or *conditioning*, where one part of an experience comes to represent in our minds the whole experience. For this woman, her depressing thoughts were anchored, or connected, to her bus journey. This woman had become conditioned automatically to think these depressing thoughts as soon as she stepped foot inside a bus.

We see a similar pattern in many other everyday behaviours. We reach out to shake hands when someone else offers theirs; we applaud at the finish of a good theatrical or musical performance; smokers usually hold their cigarette in the same hand. Each are pieces of behaviour in which we are compulsively engaged. They have been learned. Stretch your hand out to a 1-year-old and they will give you a very odd look indeed.

We asked this woman to write down her thoughts and attitude towards her behaviour and she began to realize that she could change the way she thought, that she did not need to think that way any more. She had only been thinking that way because she had done so for years.

Overcoming Our Hostility to Change

To try to get a clearer idea of why you might think change is difficult, write down in your notebook your answers to the following questions. The results might well surprise you.

1   What pain and discomfort do you expect to experience when trying to break your habit?
2   What pleasure do you get from your habit?
3   What will it cost you if you do not break your habit?
4   How would you like to look in the future, having broken this habit?
5   How would you feel about yourself if you had broken the habit?
6   List all of the pleasures you will get from having broken the habit.
7   What will you gain from being that way?
8   Describe your overall appearance and the way you feel inside.
9   How will your life be different if you don't break the habit?

This next exercise proves brilliantly how we instinctively regard change as threatening, and how the brain searches always for what is familiar and comfortable.

⊘ Interlock your fingers, with one thumb sitting on top of the other.
⊘ Notice how that feels.
⊘ It should feel normal, comfortable.
⊘ Now unlock your hands and put them back together so that the other thumb is on top. How does that feel?

- The chances are that it feels distinctly uncomfortable, as though the thumbs and two forefingers in particular are in the wrong place.
- Now go back to the other, comfortable way. This feels better, where all fingers are in the right place.

We have done this exercise with thousands of people, and every one of them, every time, without us even asking, goes for the comfortable finger-lock first. Having this kind of physical illustration of how the brain naturally directs us towards what is most comfortable, we have found, gives people an understanding of how habits form and go on, and helps them to break through old patterns of behaviour. Watch how your family, friends or colleagues sit, often in the same chair, and cross the same leg over the other.

What Habits Do for Us

- Would you agree that one of the driving forces in life is to feel good?
- Do you think the habit you are leaving behind was just one of many possible ways to feel good?
- Or does your brain still think that keeping the habit is the best way to behave?
- If we are on this Earth to feel good, what sorts of things do we try to avoid?: Pain, discomfort, unhappiness.
- How do most people move away from those experiences?
- The behaviours they adopt are smoking, doing drugs, drinking too much alcohol, etc.

⊘ Do you enjoy feeling negative, tired, lonely, stressed, bored or depressed?

⊘ What do you do when you feel this way?

With or without their habits, how many people do you know who feel good about themselves?

Perhaps not that many, but all of them can.

And because they don't feel good about themselves, they do to themselves things they perhaps would not wish on a worst enemy.

A great many people go about trying to feel better in ways that, almost invariably, eventually leave them feeling even worse.

Breaking Out of the Comfort Zone

With the feeling of comfort comes a kind of security, which is why people try at all costs to avoid change. Trying to do anything differently, whether it be crossing your legs the other way or sleeping on the other side of the bed, feels strange and uncomfortable and therefore not good, so we go back to doing whatever we did before.

For the same reason – not wanting to move outside of our comfort zone – we tend also to put the minimum amount of attention or effort into many of the things that we do.

Pete writes: When I was an aerobics instructor I would, like many others, always make my arm and leg movements as enthusiastic and energetic as possible. Rarely was this ever mirrored by any of

Every great and commanding movement in the annals of the world is the triumph of enthusiasm. Nothing great was ever achieved without it.

Ralph Waldo
Emerson

those in the many classes I instructed. Most only did the minimum they could get away with, and seemed to make their movements as conservative and low-key as possible, almost as though they were afraid of injury or running out of energy before the end of the class.

Think about the hassle most people regard getting up off the sofa to change the television channel. They are so used to having a remote control they simply cannot be bothered. Think about how impatient we are to wait longer than the few minutes it takes to microwave a ready-made meal. In each case we seem reluctant to use more than minimum effort. In order to change a habit, this reluctance needs to change, too.

Success depends on where intention is.

Gita Bellin

Practice does not make perfect. Practice makes permanent. Perfect practice makes perfect. If you really want to change, you have to practise perfectly – that is, with attention and intention.

Attention is keeping your mind on what you're doing while you're doing it. Intention is having a definite purpose that will give meaning to all your effort.

Just Try It!

The first time we try to change a habit by behaving differently, it can feel odd, uncomfortable and strange because we have stopped being, if only for a moment, the only person we know as ourselves. What we have to learn is how to come out of being what we perceive to be most comfortable, and be open to change. After all, change is really the

When confronting change, many people react in extremes. They either dig in their heels or lie down and roll over. The ability to be flexible will help you avoid these extremes, both of which are counterproductive. It will also help you to keep your balance and make a knowledgeable assessment of the value of change. You need a clear head to evaluate whether a change will have a positive or negative effect on your life.

only constant, and without it our experience of life can become dull and narrow.

You may have thought you were resistant to change, but just think, right now millions of cells are changing in your body, the season is changing, the weather is constantly changing, fashion changes. You probably aren't wearing the same style clothes as you did five years ago, you probably don't have the same hairstyle, and it is doubtful that you go to the same bars and nightclubs. Somewhere along the line you changed your mind. You can do it again. If, in your approach to breaking your habit, you can be flexible and open to change, actively seeking new ways of being, then anything is possible.

Conclusion

In many parts of the world, feeling good has become synonymous with feeling comfortable. We find and practise behaviours that serve a particular need, and believe that is as good as it gets. We don't want change because we have become too comfortable with where we are and stop looking for alternatives, even when the behaviour we have adopted has more bad effects than good. For many people there is a certain amount of pleasure in their pain, because it is familiar, habitual and in some way a comfort, and trying to change means moving away from where they are or from the person they recognize as themselves. We need to start looking for alternative ways to feel good and be open to change.

step 4

Motivation

Our business in life is not to get ahead of others, but to get ahead of ourselves; to break our own records; to outstrip our yesterday by our today.
Steward B. Johnson

How Badly Do You Want to Change?

Sten writes: I was recently coaching a group on a sports psychology course, each of whom, at the end of the first session, had to see if they could overcome one of their own phobias in order to feel confident about helping others overcome theirs. To do this, each had to handle either a snake or a large spider (both of which were tame). As the queue tailed off, I noticed one young woman looking decidedly anxious. She seemed to be trying to dodge this part of the course, but was still hanging about demonstrating a desire to tackle it without knowing exactly how.

'Are you going to do it, then?' I asked her. 'Well, I don't know,' she replied. But I knew she wanted to because she was still standing there. In order to help her and find a way round the brick wall she obviously felt she faced, I asked her what she did for a living. 'I stack supermarket shelves,' she said. The course she was on had cost more than £600, and I could tell from her accent that she had travelled quite some distance to be there. 'Big commitment,' I thought, 'she really, really wants to do this course.'

Life is not the way it's supposed to be. It's the way it is. The way you cope with it is what makes the difference.

Virginia Satir

Holding on to her obviously strong drive to complete the course, I told her that if she did, she would make a really good sports psychologist. 'Well, what is it going to be? You have done more than anyone else in this room to be here. You obviously have the resources to finish. Is this little spider going to stand between you and your dreams? Are you going to go home and admit defeat, saying to yourself: "I wish I had done it"?' I then got her to imagine what she looked like being scared of the spider, and to think about what words of encouragement she would give herself. Suddenly she said: 'I can do it.' 'Of course you can. Put your hand out and hold this hairy baby,' I said. She laughed, held her hand out, looked at the spider, looked at me, and smiled. She made the commitment and proved she could have her dream.

We all have resources to draw on which make us stronger and help us through difficult or challenging situations. Faced with what we consider to be an impossible task, we merely have to remind ourselves of a time in the past when we had to be strong, and remember that that strength is there, readily available, to be re-engaged at any moment.

Stop Giving Yourself a Hard Time

So, are you ready to change this habit? Do you know what to expect from change? If you want to see the power of the comfortable and familiar, do something different. You will notice just how strong the pull of the familiar is. When you next settle down to watch your favourite TV programme, read the newspaper or do your embroidery, sit in a different chair.

When you go to bed, sleep on the other side, or during the next week wash your hair at a different time of day than normal. When you go shopping, buy a different brand of antiperspirant or washing powder. How long can you sit with your legs crossed over differently from normal before habit moves it back? Let's see, before we start to make the changes that count, what it is like to change just a little bit. Then decide if you are ready.

Increasing Your Motivation

To look at the success of a particular gameshow host in the UK now, it is hard to believe that not so long ago he was a rather over-weight would-be celebrity working as a DJ for a small radio station, who knew that, in terms of becoming a star, he had probably missed the boat. As he sat wondering one night about what had once given him the belief that he could be a star, he began thinking about what the future held if he continued to live as he was at that time. He saw himself becoming even more overweight, with even fewer listeners than he then had, and eventually losing his job. The spiral of his life that he foresaw went ever downwards. Becoming a star was just not going to happen. He snapped, and thought: 'No, that does it. I am not going to put up with this mediocre life any longer.' He then threw away the packet of biscuits from which he had been eating, and signed up with his local gym.

Having made the decision no longer to drift into an overweight, unsuccessful middle-age, his life started to change to accommo-date the new version he foresaw for himself. His voice started to sound different on the radio, so a different type of person started to ring in. Those with whom he worked at the station reacted

There are risks and costs to a programme of action, but they are far less than the long-range risks and costs of comfortable inaction.

John F. Kennedy

Desire is the key to motivation, but it's the determined commitment to an unrelenting pursuit of your goal, a commitment to excellence, that will enable you to attain the success you seek.

Michael Jordan

differently towards him, and he started to attract attention from the people who could help him realize his reborn ambition. He accepted a number of different DJ jobs with bigger radio stations and larger numbers of listeners, until the offer to present a well-known morning gameshow came up. On the face of it no one with any ambition would have taken the job, but this man believed in himself and brought to the show his own special sort of magic. Viewers tuned in, they liked him. He has gone on to become a big star.

As we have discussed, one way to change is to turn up the pain – in other words, to think about what the future would be like should we still have our habits. Smokers might think about what would happen if they went on smoking: how their reflection in the mirror would look six months into the future, how their fingers would smell, how their lungs would feel, what their friends would say, what kind of an example they would be setting for their children and how much money they would have spent. They could take this a step further by imagining all of this a year ahead, or two years, or five. Once we have made the decision to change, it is often the serious thought of the discomfort of *not* taking action that makes us change.

When you feel motivated, it can be described as your body and mind telling you they are ready to start. You feel impelled to act to get away from or move closer to a particular set of circumstances.

Consequences of Your Actions

Pete writes: A young woman once came to see me because she wanted to stop biting her nails. This immediately brought to mind some research I had recently been reading in which the skin from beneath the fingernails of a man who used the London Underground to travel to work was taken in order for certain tests to be carried out. As well as uncovering the material the researchers were seeking, they also discovered in the sample 10 different types of faecal material, as well as a number of diseases which could only have come from animals. I said to the woman, 'Look, just stop for a moment before you bite your fingernails, and think: "Do I want to put shit in my mouth?"' Even more important than that, I told her to start thinking about how she wanted her nails to look. With help and practice, by the time I saw her a few months later she had beautiful, long fingernails.

People often do not know what it is that holds them back from making a change they strongly desire. 'I just don't seem to have the motivation to change, even though I want to,' they say to us. 'Why is that?' Yet there are other people who are so motivated by what they do that even talking about it generates in them a desire to start doing it straightaway.

How many people do you know who, so motivated by what they do, reach their potential every day of their lives? Even though we experience it periodically, most of us are not used to feeling motivated about everyday activities such as eating well, exercising, enjoying friends' company and relaxing. If we felt motivated more often, we could dramatically improve the quality of our lives. But most people associate effort with these things, and are more motivated to stay where they are. Change is often equated in our minds with pain.

Motivation is really no more than persuading yourself to do whatever it is you want to do. We have all had some experience of being motivated; we simply have to learn how to put that feeling to work in the direction we want. To do this you have to make what you want to do so compelling, and what you no longer want to do so repellent, that you want to get on and do the new thing and abandon the old NOW.

On a scale of 1 to 100, your motivation to change is probably hovering between 70 and 80. You are thinking about change, and in so doing generating and strengthening the belief that you *can* change. How about we increase that motivation further towards your goal? Motivation is, after all, nothing more than a feeling about something, and it is just as easy and effective to motivate you *away* from your habits as it is to motivate you towards the new you. In other words, turn up the pain of not taking action so it gets you to the point that you think: I have got to do something about this.

Pete writes: When I was a student I lived in a flat with four other lads. We took it in turns to cook, but always left the washing up until later. Of course, later never came, and each time we left it for another day it was like a test of each other's tolerance of the mess, to see who would give in and clear up first. Eventually the unwashed dishes were piled so high and supplies in the cupboards and drawers were so low we had to feel around in a sink full of putrid water to find a cup and teaspoon to make coffee. When the kitchen became too much of a mess and too cluttered to cook in, we started buying takeaways, so to add to the dirty dishes and unwashed cutlery there were now endless takeaway boxes. Before long the kitchen began to stink, but even though we had to walk through it to get to the bathroom, no one cleared up.

Then one night, while holding my nose to get through the kitchen to the toilet, I slipped. When I looked down I saw that the left-over food had attracted a swarm of ants and that I had slipped on one of the many slugs that covered the floor. It was that sight that finally prompted us to clean up.

Are you fed up enough with the way things are to start to change your behaviour?

Exercise to Generate Motivation to Change

You really need someone to read this exercise to you, or tape-record yourself reciting it. The first part is designed to get you to imagine what would happen if you did not change, and the second part helps you to see what life will be like once your habit has been broken.

Part 1

1   Sit comfortably.
2   Think about this habit you want to break.
3   Close your eyes and do the exercise that gets you into a relaxed and controlled state (*, page 44).
4   Think now about what would happen if you do nothing whatsoever, but go on as you are now with this habit.
5   Imagine you still have this habit in six weeks' time. Look in the mirror. Notice what you look like, sound like, smell like and feel like.
6   How do you feel about yourself? How do other people feel about you? What sort of things do you say to yourself?
7   Now take the feeling of discomfort you get from having carried on indulging your habit for another six weeks, and imagine yourself still with the habit in six months' time.

8 You have dragged with you into the future all the misery of having continued with the habit, and arrive in front of another mirror.

9 Look at yourself. See what you look like, sound like, smell like and feel like. Look at your muscle tone and your complexion. Look at the expression in your eyes.

10 How do you feel about yourself now? What do you say about yourself? What are other people saying about you?

11 Now imagine you have continued with the behaviour you want to stop for a year. All that pain, all that discomfort is magnified by another 365 days, as you look once more into the mirror.

12 Have a good look at yourself. What do you smell, sound, look and feel like?

13 What do you say to yourself? What do other people say to you? How do you feel about yourself?

14 Take that feeling and project it another five years into the future, hauling with you all the associated discomfort.

15 Now see again what you look like, sound like and feel like. Do you like what you see? Do you like what you have become? How do you feel about yourself? What does the face you see tell you about that person?

16 Now take the consequences of having behaved in that way and think about what you will be like in another 10 years, should you still have this habit.

17 Look at yourself in the mirror. Look at what you can see in that reflection and notice how you sound and feel, having continued to behave in that way for a decade. Do you like what you can see? Do other people like what they see? What do they say about you? What do you say about yourself?

18 Is that the person you want to be in 10 years' time?

Learn from yesterday, live for today, hope for tomorrow.

Stop now for a moment.

Thank yourself.

None of this has happened.

Take a couple of deep breaths, and be grateful.

You can change what has not yet occurred.

That was only an imagined future. It could happen, but it does not have to.

You get what you focus on.

Are you 100 per cent motivated to change?

If you are not ready to change your behaviour, go back and do this exercise again and again and again, until you are. Imagining the consequences of not changing is often the quickest way to decide you want to change.

If that does not work, get someone else to do the exercise with you until you are convinced you want to stop your habit. Where it will take you is so repellent that you don't even want to think about having that habit any more.

If, on the other hand, you know you are ready to change after doing this exercise, take a short break: have something to drink or go for a walk.

Having taken a sufficient rest, take four or five deep breaths before moving on to the second part of this exercise.

Part 2

1 Sit comfortably, feet flat on floor, take a few deep breaths.
2 Do the state exercise.*
3 Now think about what you will look like in six weeks' time, having made the decision to change.
4 You have not done your habit for 42 days. Look in the mirror.

5 Notice how you look, what you can hear and how it feels to be free from your habit.

6 Do you like what you see? What would you say to yourself? What do others say about you? What other changes have you made as a consequence of breaking your habit?

7 Take all of that pleasure and go six months into the future.

8 Free from the habit, you look in the mirror. Notice what you look like, sound like, smell like and feel like now you are in control and free. See how it feels to have more energy, excitement and passion.

9 What do you say to yourself? What do others say to you, having broken this habit? How do you feel about yourself?

10 You have broken the habit for a year now. Imagine arriving once again in front of a mirror.

11 Look at what you can see, hear and feel now that you are free.

12 What do you say to yourself? What are others saying about you? How do you feel now that you have broken the habit for an entire year and have moved on? What other things might you be doing? How is your life different?

13 Imagine going five years into the future. You have not had the habit for so long you can barely remember it. It is a distant memory.

14 You arrive in front of another mirror. Have a look at what you can see in the reflection, notice what you can hear and how it feels to be free and in control.

15 How do you feel about yourself? How do other people feel about you?

16 Now you are 10 years into the future, free from the habit, and you see yourself in the mirror.

You cannot teach people anything. You can only help them to discover it within themselves.
Galileo

17 Once again, be aware of what you can see, hear and feel.

18 Listen to what you say about yourself, what others say about you, and notice how it feels to have been living for 10 years without this habit. Notice how positive and powerful and in control you feel.

Now, slowly take a few deep breaths.

With each breath, breathe in that confidence you now feel. You should feel good: in control and relaxed.

Remember, you need to do these motivation exercises as many times as it takes to get you ready for change. For many people these exercises are often enough to get them to make the change. But if you are still not motivated to change, go back and do them again and again until you know that you are.

Conclusion

We believe the desire and ability to succeed is within everyone. It is like a pilot light in a boiler which grows into a big flame, depending on our motivation or feelings towards something. Going to the gym, for example, for many people means pain, effort, monotony – their pilot light is almost out. There is no motivation. For others, because of how they feel after a workout or how well they sleep when they are physically tired, they are highly motivated to go to the gym and their pilot light is in full flame.

We want the pilot light that represents your motivation to be burning bright all the time. If it is not, repeat the motivation exercises, again and again.

step 5

Beliefs

Have you ever noticed that self-belief and the ability to identify themselves with a successful person allows many successful people to do what others think they cannot? We can choose to think like a non-smoker or non-nail-biter to be able to identify with and accept that we can be that other person who does not have these habits.

Try on the idea of being this other person, have a feel for what they would feel or do in any given situation. Imagine they do not have the habit. How different from you are they? If you were them, what would you be doing instead of the habit? How different would your life be? Be that person for a day. Notice the difference, and practise noticing.

The Repetition Factor

The process of learning how to be that ex-habit person is similar to the behaviour pattern by which we developed the habit in the first place – in other words, repetition.

For example, an overweight person who thinks of themselves as fat and accepts that they are fat goes on behaving as though they are fat – in other words, eating the sorts of foods they know they should avoid. As long as they accept they are overweight and repeat the behaviour, they will be. The cycle has to be broken so that they can learn to take on life-affirming habits.

Just as every piece of fattening food confirms their view of themselves as an overweight person, every time they choose to eat healthy foods their view of themselves as a person who has control over their previously habitual behaviour is confirmed. The more examples we can generate, the more our brains will make those examples the focus of our attention.

One of the brain's many functions is to confirm what we believe. What many people often do automatically is look out for anything that substantiates their ideas about themselves and the world. So if you believe something is possible, you will create the behaviour that supports this belief. Our brains are always actively engaged in perpetuating what is happening now. It happens automatically. You choose what is happening in your head, and your brain generates more of it.

If you expect breaking your habit to be difficult, it probably will be. But when you believe you are capable of change and actually are changing, your attention is focused on this message, which reinforces the new, positive belief. Until you can believe you can break the habit, you are going to find it very

A single reason
why you can do
something is worth
a hundred reasons
why you can't.

difficult to succeed, because belief and behaviour are intrinsically linked.

Self-efficacy Beliefs

Our beliefs act as a framework for our behaviour – in other words, what you believe forms the cornerstone of how you behave and what you get. If you are in any doubt about this, think of what is known as the placebo effect. Derived from the Latin word 'I shall please', this is what takes place when patients with particular conditions are told a pill they take will cure them, even when its ingredients are little more than sugar and water. Because the patients *believe* it will help, it often does!

Described by the behavioural psychologist Paul Martin, fellow of Wolfson College, Oxford, as 'a palpable demonstration of how our psychological expectations can override the signals coming from the body', recent studies show that the placebo response can work in up to 90 per cent of cases for certain conditions, and in some instances prove more effective than the conventional medical treatment.

A whole range of reasons is given for why placebos work, but researchers agree that in all cases the mind – and more importantly our beliefs – have an effect on the body. Little research has been done so far into what is loosely known as 'mind-body medicine' or psycho-neuroimmunology, but evidence from the work done so far suggests that thoughts and emotions can trigger brain chemicals which, via the hormones and immune system, have an effect on other systems in the body. Positive emotions, for example, can help to relieve stress – and stress suppresses the production of antibodies that fight disease. So positive emotions can help to fight disease.

Dr Herbert Benson, an American physician and author of *Timeless Healing: The Power and Biology of Belief*, believes that in its memory the brain stores certain pathways to healing, or signals that stimulate the body's internal pharmacy, releasing natural healing chemicals. He believes instead of 'placebo', the phenomena should be described as 'remembered wellness'. We have conditioned the body through past behaviour to know what to do when we experience certain types of ill-health.

One of the most important aspects in aiding people's recovery from illness, according to Dr Michael Dixon, a research fellow with Exeter University and author of *The Human Effect in Medicine*, is understanding how they see the world. This can give an idea of what a patient expects will work for them. Researchers at Southampton University found, for example, that recovering from a sore throat was most effective not in the patients who had been given medication, but in those whose doctors had taken the time to listen and chat about their concerns. In another study, children who through having plasters applied to cuts learned to associate the plaster with the pain relief, would automatically feel better whenever a graze was covered with a plaster.

Another leading researcher in this field, Howard Brody of Michigan State University, says that inside our bodies each of us has healing chemical substances, the pathways of which, if stimulated in the right way, can be activated. If this is true of the way the body learns to heal itself, could it not be

The eye sees only what the mind is prepared to comprehend.

that this same type of conditioning not only locks us into habits but is also the device by which we can reverse behaviour?

Your Beliefs

Changing an habitual behaviour depends on belief, so you need to develop a way of thinking that will help you to believe you can behave differently. To do this easily you need *self-efficacy* – beliefs that support your aim. Derived from the word *efficacious*, meaning 'producing the desired result', and first coined by the psychologist Albert Bandura, self-efficacy means you believe you can achieve a particular objective and know you have the resources to do so (just as we perhaps subconsciously do during the placebo effect).

In research Dr Bandura carried out into how self-belief can affect performance, he concluded that a person's beliefs about themselves could predict far more accurately how they would perform in the future than anything they had achieved in the past. No matter how many times you have failed in the past, believe you can succeed and you will. Change your map of the world. The world is changing all the time.

People with high perceived self-efficacy try more, accomplish more and persist longer at a task than those with low perceived self-efficacy. Bandura speculates that this is because those with high perceived self-efficacy tend to have more control over their environment, and therefore experience less uncertainty. But perceived self-efficacy may not correspond to real self-efficacy. If you really believe you cannot do something, you will find a way of keeping that change from occurring.

There is but one cause of human failure and that is man's lack of faith in his true Self.

William James

People are always blaming circumstances for what they are. I do not believe in circumstances. The people who get on in this world are the people who get up and look for the circumstances they want, and if they cannot find them, make them.

George Bernard Shaw

When the Wright brothers first got their plane off the ground, they did not really believe what they had done. Powered flight was then deemed impossible. So they decided to keep it a secret for a while until they were comfortable with the idea that they had flown and could easily do so any time they wanted. They went on to make dozens of flights up and down a particular field, and when they were ready sent a letter to one of the scientific magazines saying they had achieved powered flight. After it was published, the magazine was bombarded with letters from readers accusing the Wright brothers of being liars because powered flight was not possible. None of them had seen the plane in action, yet because of strongly held beliefs they could not bring themselves to imagine that someone had made possible what they believed to be impossible. It later emerged that one of the main complainants had been a neighbour of the Wright brothers who, every day, drove past the field where they had done their practice flights. He must physically have witnessed the plane flying overhead on a number of occasions, but because he so vehemently believed it was not possible, the belief overrode what he had seen with his own eyes.

What Do You Believe?

The difference between those who can break a habit and those who have failed in the past is that the former will look constantly for ways in which to reinforce their belief in themselves without the habit, whereas the latter will either lower their expectations or blame others or forces beyond their control for their inability to change.

Just trust yourself,
then you will know
how to live.

Goethe

Developing Self-efficacy

Perhaps with a record of past failure, many people have difficulty making themselves believe they can break a habit. But
there are a number of ways to achieve self-belief or, more
importantly, beliefs about your abilities in certain situations.

One particular man who came to us for help said he found it hard to
believe he could change his behaviour. We got him to write down
every time in his life when he had given 100 per cent to some project, overcome obstacles to achieve, or was given great praise. We
then asked him to close his eyes and imagine, as if in a cinema sitting in a soft and comfortable chair, watching himself on a film going
through each of these experiences. We told him to observe himself
excelling in each of the instances he could remember, making the
screen as large, the colour as bright and the volume as loud as he
liked. 'Feel what it is like,' we said, 'watch yourself doing these
things.' By practising this mini-movie and recapturing that feeling of
success and achievement, it was not long before he believed he was
capable of almost anything, including breaking his habit.

Techniques and
technologies are
important. But
adding trust is
the issue of the
decade.

Tom Peters

Some research has suggested that many of the people at the
top of their professions strongly believe that they are better
than they really are. But this belief allows them to BE better
than they really are. And the more successful they are, the
more evidence there appears to be to support their belief in
their greatness.

Most people never realize their potential because they do
not realize they have any. Success in many societies often
goes unrewarded or even ignored, so we tend not to remember
how we achieved it.

The beliefs that you hold about yourself in relationship to your skills and abilities and the environment in which you live will determine how successful you will be. These beliefs can be as helpful or unhelpful as you like.

Let's say, for example, that when playing sport you always give 100 per cent. You have always done this, and know that you are capable of giving all at any level of play. In holding this belief about yourself when thinking about your performance at a forthcoming competition, you can imagine yourself working your very hardest, giving everything, from how you train to what you eat and how much rest you take.

You rehearse the event in your mind, over and over, knowing you will be at your best.

As you think about the competition in great detail, your brain begins to act on the plan, and when the time comes for the plan to be executed, the brain knows no other way of dealing with the situation other than what you have mentally and physically rehearsed. You know and believe that in sport you always give 100 per cent, so your brain generates the behaviour to support the belief. When the event is over, you look back and see how well you did, adding further to your belief in yourself.

The brain tends to look for confirmed evidence such as this, so the more evidence you can provide to substantiate your belief – whatever it is – the clearer the direction is for the unconscious mind.

Pete writes: I once worked with a cricket team whose players had placed on themselves, almost without knowing, performance limitations. One player in particular did not believe he was capable of completing 100 runs without being bowled out. Whenever asked,

Men are not prisoners of fate, but only prisoners of their own minds.
Franklin D. Roosevelt

his reply was always along the lines of: 'Well, I'm not so sure. I have made 50 runs before, but I just can't imagine myself scoring 100.' The cricketer constantly spoke to himself negatively about his ability to score 100, and his behaviour confirmed his belief, because he never did.

Pete writes: A woman came to see me once because she wanted to give up smoking. She had tried before, she told me, and always failed because it was too difficult and she had no willpower. She did not believe, based on past evidence, that she could. Before she went on, I asked her if she could imagine herself in the future not smoking. She said she could not. I told her she would find it difficult to break the habit if she could not even imagine herself being able to break it.

To help her to build a belief, I asked her to remember and tell me about all the times in her life when she had persisted at something. She said she managed to learn to drive and pass her test at 25. Had she ever considered giving up, even though she was older than many who learn and find it difficult? I asked. No, she replied. She also told me about how she managed to study and complete a degree while married with two children, and how she had been there to help a friend through a period of serious illness.

I then asked her to imagine making a movie of these experiences so she could watch herself as though it was a film on a large screen. 'I am doing this,' I told her, 'because I want you to realize how capable you really are and to start believing that you can give up smoking.' She imagined the movie, which as soon as it ended began again, over and over and over. With each screening the movie became more real and, when she had watched for a while, she felt good about herself. I then asked her what she would say about the person in the movie. After some thought, she said: 'They are hot, they can do anything.' Then I told her to make

Life is a movie you see through your own unique eyes. It makes little difference what's happening out there. It's how you take it that counts.

*Denis Waitley,
The Winner's Edge*

the statement her own, so 'They can do anything' became 'I can do anything'. Repeating this affirmation, she then imagined the movie again, only this time she stepped into it and made it even more dramatic, like an Indiana Jones or a James Bond film. I told her to watch herself as the star and, whenever the movie finished, to start it from the beginning again straightaway. On each replay the colour, sound and acting qualities were enhanced further and further, so the events were as real as when they had actually occurred.

This exercise put her into a really powerful state and gave her the foundation of the belief that she really could stop smoking. Once she had been able to remember and again believe she could do anything, she was able to stop.

When you go to see a movie, particularly an action film, the director is trying to give you an experience through all of your senses. Much the same thing is happening with the next exercise: you are making up an experience that just happens to be true. As well as proving to you just how capable you are, we will also develop from this exercise an affirmation – a positive statement about yourself you know to be true, which will help you to achieve your goal.

Building a Powerful Belief

If you truly believe you can break your habit, you act in ways that support the belief. The next exercise is designed to help you build the belief that you can change.

You might find doing the second part of this exercise easier with your eyes closed and with someone else reading it out to you, or you could tape-record it for yourself.

Part one

1 Get your notebook and, giving yourself plenty of time with perhaps some music playing in the background, write down as many instances as you can of times in your life when you:
   – performed well at a task
   – were praised for a task
   – persisted in the face of obstacles or difficulties
   – gave 100 per cent to some project
   – learned and mastered a new skill.

   It could be any moment, and the event could be or might seem to be trivial. One of our earliest memories of a moment of achievement is being able to tie shoelaces, but it could be anything: the way you work, how you keep your house in order, what you do as a hobby, the way you dealt with a potentially self-damaging situation, the day you passed your driving test or bought a house or tiled the bathroom.

   Take time to recall and write down all the events you can remember. It does not matter if it takes a few days. Aim to have about 30 on your list.

2 When you have a nice long list, read them all through as though it were a list of achievements of someone you have never met.

3 Now choose the five of which you are most proud. These are the ones that, when you think about them, give you the best feeling.

4 Arrange them in your mind so one event can follow another (not necessarily in chronological order), almost like a movie or documentary of which you are the director.

Part two

5 Now, sit comfortably and get into state* (page 44)

6 Imagine you are sitting in the cinema and about to start watching a film in which you are starring. It is a film about those five experiences all put together.

7 Watch the film on a big screen in front of you slowly from beginning to end, taking particular note of how you perform in the starring role.

8 Make what you are looking at bigger by doubling the size of the screen, and give the movie house surround sound.

9 Notice how good it feels to watch yourself on this huge screen in full colour in those moments of achievement.

10 As it ends, let the movie start over again so that it never actually finishes, and each time it begins the quality of the colour and sound become better and better and the film is brighter, sharper and clearer.

11 Scrutinize each event and notice how it feels, looks and sounds to watch that you on the big screen.

12 Think about how well that you has done, how much energy that you puts into each of those experiences.

13 As the film starts again, the picture is even larger and the volume is even greater. Repeat this at least five times.

14 Now stop.

15 Take a few deep breaths and bring your attention back to wherever you are.

Now do a critique: what would you say were among the qualities of the person you were watching? Would you give this person an Oscar for their performance? If not, go back and do it again, even if you have to go overboard and make up some of the situations.

Once they have given an award-winning performance, answer the following questions:

What would you say about this person? What are their qualities?
Are they persevering, no matter what?
Are they determined and focused on what they want?
Are they dedicated to self-improvement?
Are they really positive and filled with self-belief?

Write down the qualities you attribute to them. Make what you have written into a really powerful statement, such as 'They are really positive', 'They are very focused', 'They can do anything', 'They have got what it takes'.

Now we want you to get out of the director's chair and step into this Oscar-winning performance while repeating the statement. But instead of saying: 'They are really positive' say 'I am really positive', so your statement becomes a personal affirmation.

1 Now get back into state*.
2 Instead of sitting in the director's chair, step inside to take the lead role in your film and feel what it is like to experience those events all over again.
3 See what you saw, listen out for what you heard, and feel what it was like to achieve success in each instance.

4   Each time you go over this amazing feature-length film, feel how good it is in each of those events.

5   Repeat your affirmation to yourself, for example, 'I am always in control'. Say it as though you mean it, feeling the words inside your body as though you were shouting them from the rooftops.

6   Make the movie more real each time – brighter, bolder, clearer, louder – and go through it at least five times. It must be as though it never ends; it is just a continuous movie.

7   Then take a few deeper breaths before slowly bringing your attention back to where you are.

If you are not convinced that you deserve an Oscar for that performance, do the exercise again. You can have as many takes as you like to perfect your performance and your realization that you have the power to change.

Once you know you can, think:

What was it about you then that helped you to succeed?
Were you motivated?
Were you confident?
Did you believe you could achieve?

Repeat the sentence you chose for yourself as the film critic:

'I persevere no matter what' or 'I am determined and focused on what I want.'

Say it aloud, with conviction, and mean it.

This is your affirmation. Repeat it to yourself at least 100 times a day, always like you mean it.

> When the heart weeps for what it has lost, the spirit laughs for what it has found.
> *sufi aphorism*

Make a note now in your notebook of the affirmation, as we will be using it in some of the other exercises. We would also like you to get into the habit of saying it to yourself whenever you feel your self-belief beginning to ebb, or when you want to be particularly effective or just more positive about your ability to achieve. It could be anything. Don't worry if it feels silly at first or you don't really believe it. Repeat it enough and you will. The more you use it, the better you will become at using it.

What you are doing is drawing on the resources you already have which, in the past, helped you to achieve success. What you should have realized is that you are far more resourceful than you think.

Now that you have watched and starred in the movie a few times, how do you feel?

With that feeling, think of some of the challenges that lie ahead along the habit-breaking path. Do they seem like problems to the person whose achievements you have relived? You should be able to contemplate and face the challenges ahead with considerably more ease than before you sat down to make that list.

Mini Exercise

Write down your affirmation in colour on a few pieces of paper and stick them up in places where you will see them regularly each day. Whenever you see the affirmation, repeat it out loud to yourself a few times as though saying it from the top of a mountain or shouting it from the rooftops.

A Belief Needs Legs to Get Going

To help create belief in yourself, you could also look at the belief as an idea. For many of you the belief might still be just a nice idea. How prepared for change are you? What are you prepared to do that will support your belief? Like a table that needs legs to stand, we need references on which our beliefs can rest. What are the references that are going to make your idea stand up?

Let us say the idea is that you could be slimmer. You have a HABIT of being overweight but an IDEA of being slimmer. One reference is to change what you eat, another to be prepared to exercise, another to eat more slowly, another to drink more water. Now that your idea has four legs, it can stand. But if you stop using one of them, the belief starts to fall over, so you need to think of what else you can do to make it stand again. You could eat more fruit and vegetables and/or cut down on the desserts. Suddenly you have a very strong foundation on which to support your belief.

What about your ideas about your habit? What efforts can you make that will make your idea of breaking your habit stand up and turn into a really powerful conviction that you can succeed?

step **6**

The New You

The snow goose need not bathe to make itself white. Neither need you do anything but be yourself.

Lao-Tse

Writing Your Script for the Future

Have you noticed that some actors are so good at playing a role that you forget they are acting at all? Many of the best spend huge amounts of time getting into a part, thinking about how the character would think, feel, act and move through the world. We know we are not born with habits; we practise them, just like an actor learning a new role. All that we are trying to do now is to teach you how to break that habit and play a different version of yourself.

Pete writes: I once worked with a doctor who smoked. He had smoked for many years and it had, in the past, helped him at times of stress and anxiety to cope with the huge number of sick people with whom he had to deal. He admitted, however, that the smoking no longer gave him the relief or enjoyment it once had, and he felt guilty about the sort of example he was setting his patients. When he came to see me I suggested he spend some time imagining and

A long life may not be good enough, but a good life is long enough.

Benjamin Franklin

pretending that he had never actually smoked. I told him to assume the identity of who he was without the cigarettes. A month after he had given up I asked him if it had been hard. 'It is pointless asking me that,' he said. 'It is as if I never have.' .

Simply imagining an event or great experience has an effect on the body. In an experiment conducted for a science-based television programme, a group of people were told to regularly imagine doing exercise. Although the difference was tiny, small muscle definition was detected a few weeks later, and all the control group had used to change their body shape was their minds.

This might sound crazy, even unbelievable, but if we think about it, the nervous system that connects the whole body starts in the brain, which sends messages to and collects messages from the rest of the body. It actually makes sense that what happens in one will have an effect in the other.

Research on sportsmen and -women using a biofeedback machine has also shown that as they *imagine* themselves competing, so their heart rate, blood pressure and body temperature rise, as if they were actually competing physically. As this is the case, the potential for using our own imaginations in this way is enormous.

Before the 400-metre hurdles race in 1993 in which Sally Gunnell broke the world record, she spent months and months winning the race in her head. In minute detail she saw herself at the start-line, then setting off, running the race and then crossing the finish line first. She went over and over the experience in her head, time and time again, so that every time she imagined the race, it was as though she were actually there, running it. She later said, after breaking the world record, that for a minute or two after the race she had not been sure whether she really had won it or whether it had been in her imagination. So many times had she been over the race in her head in the months before the race, convincing herself she was going to win, that she could barely tell the difference between the real race and the imagined one.

Snap Shots

Prince Naseem Hamed, a famous British boxer, has been able in the past to predict the round in which he was going to win a fight. Many people think he is arrogant, having the cheek before a fight to say at which point he will win it. But the reason he says this is quite simple: he has thought about the fight in so much detail, over and over, round by round, minute by minute, second by second, that he convinces himself of what he is going to do before it has happened.

How about that movie of your own success? We can make it into a blockbuster, with absolutely no expense spared. In the movie you have broken your habit. You are strong and in control. Some people find this difficult, but remember you are making this up. It lets you use your imagination. And if you don't get it right first time, you have the budget to make changes.

1   *Get into state.
2   Think of five scenarios in the future in which you are free from your habit.

3 Imagine these five experiences as pictures or snapshots in front of you.

4 Take the first one and see it moving closer to you until it is big enough to fill a large screen.

5 Look at yourself in the future, free from your habit, confident, positive and in control. Watch yourself carefully.

6 Make the picture clearer, brighter and bolder.

7 After 30 seconds, push the image back and repeat this process with each of the other four pictures.

8 Now, one at a time, allow each picture to move towards you until it moves inside you. Step into it for 30 seconds, feeling what it is like in the future to be in control and taking on the new way of behaving.

9 Do this with each snapshot, stepping in and out for 30 seconds, making sure each time that you make the experiences clearer and more real to you.

10 Finally, when you have done this with all the experiences, bring them all together, and step into the entire event like it is an ongoing movie, with one future event following another. When it ends just start it again, making it even better. Keep going over it several times.

11 When you watch the film see yourself clearly, as though the future has already passed and you are watching a video recording. It must be as though the achievement has already happened, and there is nothing you can do about it. Your mind will then know the direction in which you want to go.

Doing this exercise once is rarely enough. You would not expect an actor to read a script through once to really get into the part. Go over and over it until you convince yourself

Nobody gets to
live life backwards.
Look ahead, that is
where your future
lies.
Ann Landers

you are that future you. Make it like Sally Gunnell, so that
when it comes to imagining these events, you feel as though
you are already there. You can, if you think you can.

Assumptions

The secret of
happiness is not in
doing what one
likes, but in liking
what one has to
do.
James Barrie

Often people will make assumptions about trying to break a
habit, for example that it is going to be difficult – and then
they cannot do it. If you truly expect something to be difficult,
it will be. The pain we associate with our past experience of
trying to give up a habit and failing makes us recoil from
change and believe that any future attempt will be difficult.
This assumption is not going to help you to succeed.

If a man lives
without inner
struggle, if
everything
happens in him
without opposition
... he will remain
such as he is.
G. I. Gurdjieff

Those who manage to change their behaviour do go
through some surprising realizations. Some come to enjoy,
for example, the feeling of wrenching the power over their
lives back from a packet of cigarettes or a box of chocolates.
They do not think: 'Oh, I have tried it before and it didn't
work, so there is no point in trying again.' They leave behind
what was in the past, change their approach, their expectations and their beliefs, and their behaviour changes too.

The best thing
about the past?
It's over, it's not
happening any
more!
Richard Bandler

Historical Heroes

**Pete writes: Some years ago I met a West Indian cricketer who
was forever traumatized while playing by a bad experience in the
past. Whenever he went out to play, he remembered his mistakes**

Even Archibald Leech wants to be Cary Grant.

Cary Grant – real name Archibald Leech

Life can only be understood backwards; it has to be lived forwards.

Soren Kierkegaard

in the past and, as a consequence, never played that well. I asked him to make a picture in his head of a cricket player he truly admired. It happened to be a very famous one named Viv Richards. I then told him to imagine being that person whenever he was about to play. By doing this he was able to play better than he had ever played before, and became so good at assuming the Viv Richards role that halfway through a match when someone called his name, he did not answer to it, so immersed was he in his hero's personality.

Most of us have heroes, people we've learned about at school or college whom we come to admire. Sten's hero is Juan Fangio, the Argentine Grand Prix racing driver, who won a string of world champion titles in the 1950s. Whenever faced with a dilemma, Sten always tries to imagine what his hero would say or do. We can use these people we admire to help us through periods of temptation.

1   *Get into state.
2   Is there an historical or contemporary figure you particularly admire or to whom you can relate?
3   Make a picture of them and imagine they are standing in front of you.
4   See and feel the texture of their clothes and shoes, notice the shape of their body and, when you can see them in as much detail as possible, step inside them and feel what it is like to live out that role.
5   It is just another role, in exactly the same say as you've lived out your role as a smoker/overeater/procrastinator or whatever.

The winners in life think constantly in terms of 'I can', 'I will' and 'I am'. The losers, on the other hand, concentrate their waking thoughts on what they should have or would have done, or what they can't do.

Denis Waitley

6 Sensations often begin with the hands: what are they doing? Feel what this feels like.

7 Once you have a really strong feeling of how it is to be this other person, imagine what they would do if faced with the same or a similar difficulty to the one you have right now.

8 How would they behave?

9 What would their advice be to another person in that situation?

10 How would they break a habit?

11 What would they do instead?

12 Once you have some useful information, thank them and step out, back into you. Take a few deep breaths.

step 7
Making Mistakes

We learn wisdom from failure much more than from success; we often discover what will do, by finding out what will not do; and probably he who never made a mistake never made a discovery.
Samuel Smiles

What would you attempt to do if you knew you could not fail?
Dr Robert Schuller

What do you think was the most natural thing you've ever had to learn? How do we learn new things? Think about how you learned to walk, ride a bicycle or drive a car, or acquire any other new skill. Often you got it wrong a great many times before, finally, you got it right.

Let's start with walking. Learning how to get it right is an act of perpetually falling over, yet when we learned, we were not conscious of continual failure. We simply got back up on our feet and tried again, and again and again, until we could walk. At no point does a baby, because he or she keeps falling, think: 'Oh well, I may as well give up.' The natural and inherent desire to succeed is so strong that it compels the baby to keep on and on trying.

What if we all had that 'Oh, I cannot be bothered, I give up' attitude towards learning to walk? We would probably all be crawling round on the floor. Did you give up learning to ride a bike when you fell off, or quit trying to learn how to drive when you stalled? Probably not. As we grow up we tend to become more self-conscious and unwilling to make

When I was young I observed that nine out of ten things I did were failures. I didn't want to be a failure, so I did ten times more work.
George Bernard Shaw

mistakes, and when we do make one, we give ourselves such a hard time that we fear ever making another. But often, that is the only way to learn.

We All Make Them, We All Have Them

Big mistakes are only big lessons if you make them yourself.

Many people believe that mistakes reveal their weaknesses. Often professional sportspeople do not like admitting, even to themselves, that they have any weaknesses. But if we choose to ignore them, what happens? They resurface at the most trying of times and can often bring us down. Just one mistake, for many, is sufficient excuse to throw in the towel. How much better and more productive to learn from and even mentally correct our mistakes. If you have time to think about throwing in the towel, you also have the time to think about success. Which do you think is more worth making the focus of your life?

A step in the wrong direction is better than staying on the spot all your life. Once you're moving forward you can correct your course as you go. Your automatic guidance system cannot guide you when you're standing still.
Maxwell Maltz

Pete writes: One particular squash player I agreed to coach invited me to watch him play. On the day in question I arrived late, so he did not know when I was there. Very quickly I noticed that while his good shots went seemingly unnoticed, he 'rewarded' bad shots with angry verbal abuse and continuous cursing. I asked him about this after his game. 'Does getting angry with yourself make you play any better?' I asked. The answer he gave is probably obvious. 'Well,' I said, 'instead of cursing yourself after each bad shot, stop for a moment and remember yourself hitting the ball correctly.' He tried this technique repeatedly, and before long it started to work and he became a far superior player. He

If you find a path with no obstacles, it probably doesn't lead anywhere. When you get into a tight place and everything goes against you till it seems as though you could not hold on a minute longer, never give up then, for that is just the place and time that the tide will turn.

Harriet Beecher Stowe

The illiterate of the next decade will not be individuals who cannot read and write, but the ones who cannot learn, unlearn and relearn.

Everyone is the architect of their own learning.

said to me later: 'This is so easy and feels so good that it almost seems as though I am cheating.'

I also worked with a top goalkeeper who, like the squash player, would give himself a hard time when he failed to save a goal. He would go over and over the mistake in his head, which naturally made him feel even worse. I suggested a very easy but radically effective technique: After having made a mistake, instead of replaying the error repeatedly in his head, I told him to imagine having saved the goal. By replacing the memory of failure with success over and over, his brain would soon know which behaviour he wished to adopt.

If after each mistake or lapse as you break this habit you can go over the situation and remember yourself not making the mistake or lapse, the chances are that, when faced with a similar set of circumstances, you won't make the same mistake again. Your unconscious will start to follow the new roadmap of what you consciously know you want to do.

Remember earlier when we talked about the pilot light? The flame flares brightly when we feel motivated to do something, and is dim when we lack motivation. Many people who decide to break a habit and who are motivated spend time thinking about life being different. They have developed a belief that they can change. Any of us can fall by the wayside by slipping back into old habits.

Anyone who has experienced success knows how to master failure. Failing is part of succeeding and mistakes are mishaps, not crises. Acknowledge them, correct them, and then let them go. Do not let them govern or sabotage your new life. Successful people only ever see things working out. To them, a mistake is an opportunity.

You will have wonderful surges forward. Then there must be a time of consolidating before the next forward surge. Accept this as part of the process and never become downhearted.
Eileen Caddy, God Spoke to Me

Take heart, truth and happiness will get you in the end. You can't lose in this game. Have fun. It goes on too long to be taken seriously all the time.
John and St Clair Thomas, Eyes of the Beholder

If there were no difficulties, there would be no triumphs.

Monty Roberts, otherwise known as the Horse Whisperer, did some work with businesses. He would often be able to turn them from failing companies into highly successful institutions. When asked his secret, he said the most important lesson was in teaching the staff who worked at these companies to make mistakes. It was the only way they learned how not to repeat them, he said.

In fact, when you make a mistake, laugh, especially if you don't feel like it. Doing that alone releases seratonin, which is what is known as the 'feeling of wellbeing' chemical. You cannot hold on to depressing or self-defeating thoughts when the corners of your mouth are up-turned. Try it – it is impossible. To keep your attitude to your progress – and any slip-ups that occur along the way – in proportion, smile.

Dealing with Difficulty

Preparing to fail sounds very negative, but you need to be armed with the ability to avoid temptation if you want to succeed in changing your habit.

Plan to have knock-backs, because they do and will happen. How you deal with them will determine how successful you will be in breaking your habit. Expect adversity, but factor in perseverance.

Spend as much time as you can thinking about and planning your reaction to hiccups or potential knock-backs along the way. Think about what it will be like to be offered a cigarette, for example, or to feel like putting off some important

As a man thinks,
so does he
become. Every
man is the son of
his own works.
Cervantes

The best way to
escape from a
problem is to solve
it.

It is not because
things are difficult
that we do not
dare; it is because
we do not dare
that they are
difficult.
Seneca

task or being stressed when faced with a pile of work. How are you going to deal with those situations?

While you perceived change as a problem, you were placing yourself at a disadvantage. Many people grow up regarding anything that gets in their way as an obstacle, a nuisance, a problem they cannot surmount, and move away from or try to avoid it. Doing this, though, will take you in the opposite direction from where it is you want to go – in other words, away from being able to change your habit.

Rather than seeing whatever change it is you want to make as a problem, regard it is a personal challenge, and instead of focusing on or thinking so much about which part of the change is a problem, focus instead on the result of the change. What will you be like once you have achieved it? The change should feel much closer.

step  8

Saying Goodbye to Old Habits

What Makes People Think They Cannot Change?

The last 99.9 per cent of success is working like the devil to keep your spirits up during the inevitable storms. Learn something new every day and practise that something, awkward or not and no matter what, until it has become part of your nature.

We do not see things as they are. We see them as we are.
The Talmud

The way we view the world and everything in it is based on our experiences in the past. Our expectations of the future are formed by what we already know. We are products of what we have experienced and, perhaps subconsciously, come to believe nothing can ever be any different.

Most of us see not what is really there, but what we perceive to be there in terms of our own past experience. We can judge people's appearance and behaviour purely in terms of our own experience of whom they might remind us of, or we might regard a particular activity on the basis of our own experience of it.

Can it really be that we have become so practised at doing what we have always done that we are able to condition ourselves into thinking we are this person or that person, and never have a choice in how we define ourselves?

> Every thought you have makes up some segment of the world you see. It is with your thoughts, then, that we must work, if your perception of the world is to be changed.
>
> *A Course in Miracles*

People all over the world are running over the same patterns of thought and behaviour again and again. It's one of the main functions of our brains: to save time by making short-cuts, grouping things together into sets and generalizing the content of those sets.

Time for a break = time for a cigarette.
Cup of tea = and a biscuit.
Watch a good film = start biting nails.

This is the habit that makes all other habits possible. Most of the time this way of behaving serves us well. We know when we hear the sound of an approaching fire engine that it is time to get out of the road, for example, or that when a partner or friend uses a particular tone of voice, we need to pay attention.

As soon as you start to notice your responses, you can start to choose. The one habit that will let you change all other habits is the habit of noticing how automatic many of our choices are, and then choosing to do something different.

A few days after one of our workshops we got a phone call from a woman who had been there telling us about a change in attitude she had had, and how it was affecting not just her but the people round her. 'This guy I work with was always able to wind me up. I started to notice what he was doing, and my own response, and it really made me think. So when he started at me again the other day I just said: "If you want an argument you'll be having it with someone else because I'm happy the way I am, thank you." You should have seen the look on his face – it was as though time was standing still.'

We all cling to the past, and because we cling to the past we become unavailable to the present.

Bhagwan shree Rajneesh, Walking in Zen, Sitting in Zen

Start to notice the repetitive and cyclical nature of your own and others' communication and behaviours. You will quickly know which bits to change. Instead of going to the trouble of merely breaking an unwanted habit, choose a new one that serves you better. Get into the habit of saying: 'I'm not going to do *that* when I could do *this*' – and doing it!

Attitude and Emotions

With whatever we have experienced in the past comes an attitude and an expectation. We don't recollect a good party or a bad day at the office without also remembering how we reacted, both mentally and emotionally. Perhaps when recalling the party our spirits are lifted, as they were when we were there, or when remembering that particularly bad day at work we feel as downcast as we did on the day. When anticipating either circumstance again, there is every chance that these emotional and mental responses will resurface.

When people think about the last time they tried to break a habit and failed, they may feel depressed and defeatist, even drained. When people do not succeed, they condition themselves into believing that any future attempt will be no different.

In our experience there are three different types of sportsmen and -women: the brilliant, the OK, and the mediocre. Ask the first if they can remember a great sporting moment and they come alive. As they recount it they are right there in the memory, reliving every aspect of every moment. Ask them if they can recall a bad moment, and it has been pushed back so far in their memory that they struggle even to understand the question. The OK sportsmen and -women can recall good and bad moments in more or less equal measure, while the mediocre seem to prefer to relive their bad memories in every detail than recall their greatest achievements.

What is the difference between these three types? They have filtered what has happened to them differently. The brilliant sportspeople have put all bad experiences well and truly behind them, and can almost immediately reharness how it feels to be at their best doing their best. For the mediocre, their best is no more than a very distant memory, so enveloped are they by their failings and failures.

Why do you think so few people in life truly excel? Consider the men and women who reach the pinnacle of business and commerce, or those who top the music charts, the actors and actresses who consistently obtain the best parts, or those in sport with more than one Olympic gold. Why is it there are only a handful at the top of their respective professions? The difference between those who make it and those who don't is the same as that which distinguishes those who succeed in breaking their habits and those who fail. That difference, we believe, is an attitude that accepts nothing short of complete success.

Because so many of us have failed in the past at changing a habit, we need to learn how to change the emotional and mental responses we attach to trying. If instead of feeling a sense of impending failure when contemplating the breaking of a habit we can learn to associate thinking about and making that change with a sense of success and achievement, our motivation to and belief that we can succeed will

Life is what it is,
you cannot change
it, but you can
change yourself.
*Hazrat Inayat
Khan*

Whatever the
conscious mind
thinks and
believes, the
subconscious
identically creates.
*Brian Adams,
How to Succeed*

automatically increase. We can learn to see, think and expect in different ways, just like those who reach the top do all the time.

Why should you not be able to change your expectations about yourself in a way you want that is not based on past failure or an inability to do so? Changing has as much to do with how you think about yourself as it does with what you do.

One young woman we worked with told us how she would stand on the scales each night, expecting to have put on weight even though she ate sensibly and exercised regularly. As she approached the scales, she would feel a sense of dread, of failure and of being fat. Her failed efforts to become slim in the past had created in her a lack of self-belief, and so any future attempts were tainted by all the feelings and thoughts she had then experienced. We told her that if she were going to weigh herself regularly, to get on the scales expecting to have lost weight, to feel the same sense of exhilaration and excitement as when she'd last reached a goal, and to say to herself with confidence: 'I feel fitter, slimmer and better.' In time, having practised with conviction, she became just that.

Think again of the person you would like to be. Picture that self. Now, would he or she have whichever habit it is you have? Probably not. Our self-image can make a huge difference. If you perceive yourself as someone who smokes, you probably think you always will. It is personal myth. When you can learn the habit of thinking of yourself as a non-smoker, you have a far better chance of becoming one.

How We Know Change Is Possible

Believe it or not, you can start to make quite massive differences fairly quickly. Spend the next day looking up as much as you can. When we look down, we tend to feel down: by looking up our spirits are also lifted.

A friend of ours used this technique on a client who would not respond to direct instructions, by telling her such a fascinating story about chimneys that the client went away with the intention of paying them more attention. On her next appointment the client said she had had a fantastic week and felt wonderful. She then went on to share her observations on the chimneys in the area where she lived. What the client had not realized was that, simply by looking up more often than down, she felt much better.

Your Views on the World

As an exercise, we ask those who attend our workshops to write down in as much detail as possible everything they see when they hear the phrase: 'The cat sat on the mat.' Try it yourself, and get a few friends or colleagues to do likewise, and you will probably be amazed at the enormous differences in the descriptions. The mats and cats are usually incredibly diverse, as are their settings.

This exercise or game is merely an illustration of the amazing differences in all of our views, both of and on the world. The differences just six words can produce is, in our experience,

I sometimes need to step out of the picture and check what I've done and where I want to go before stepping back in.

Ricky Martin

always staggering. But what happens when that is translated into whole decades of experience? It is only when we think about this that we can begin to appreciate how very different our outlooks are.

The human mind's amazing ability to translate our experiences into representations of objective reality is what makes the world seem as difficult or as easy a place to be as we go on to convince ourselves it is. What if you could change those representations, so that your beliefs about how difficult it is to stop your habit are also altered?

Really, life is simple, but we have made it complicated. Making it simple again takes a little work. Why? Because we have practised thinking that it is complicated for so long. Many people are habitually looking for mistakes in themselves and other people; they don't take care of themselves and settle for second best. The successful people do what everyone else does not do. They go that little bit further. They pull out all the stops. So can you.

Switch

As we've said, people generally tend to see themselves very negatively; in a recent report, only 1 per cent of women said they were content with themselves. We ask people during our workshops to shout about what they are good at, and most of them struggle. It is only by learning how to see yourself positively, by seeing what you *have* rather than what you do not have, that you will ever be able to achieve even half of what you are capable of achieving.

Accept the challenges so that you can feel the exhilaration of victory.

George S. Patton

Looking at yourself from the outside can help in getting some perspective on yourself and your behaviour.

A famous recording artist was seen by millions some time ago having one of the most childish tantrums ever thrown by an adult on television. A few months later, while being interviewed for a magazine article, he was asked about the incident. 'Well yes,' he said. 'There haven't been any more of those. It's amazing what seeing yourself behave badly on TV can do.'

- ⊘ Imagine someone else on TV having your habit.
- ⊘ What do they look like?
- ⊘ What would you say to them that would help them change?
- ⊘ Now give yourself the same advice, and follow it.

This next exercise is designed to help you to see yourself the way you want to be rather than focusing on how you do not want to be.

1   *Get into state.
2   Most computers have Microsoft Windows, and if you are familiar with this you will know that on the top right-hand corner of each document there are three boxes: one containing a little line, which when clicked makes the document disappear to the bottom of the screen; another which when activated enlarges the document to fill the screen; the third with the X which closes the document down.
3   Visualize yourself on this type of screen, with the three boxes, engaged in your habit.

4 Now click on the little line at the top of the screen and watch it disappear.

5 Now click on the box with the square and watch as it pops up to fill the screen.

6 This document contains you engaged in your new behaviours.

7 Watch it for a while.

8 Then go back to the beginning, with your habit on the screen, and go through the process again; minimize the old habit and open up your new behaviour.

9 Repeat this as many times as you can.

You can also do this exercise another way, particularly if you are not familiar with computers.

1 Get into state.*

2 See yourself engaging in your habit on a big cinema screen. Your new behaviour is on the tiny screen of a hand-held portable television.

3 As fast as you can, switch the pictures round, so the behaviour you wish to adopt is big and bold, while that you wish to drop is barely visible on the hand-held TV, so that with a flick of a finger, you can turn it off.

4 Repeat the switch again and again.

Mini Exercise

When you are feeling particularly tired, perhaps during the course of a working day, stop whatever it is you are doing – this need take no longer than a minute. Either seated or standing, close your eyes. Straighten your back, keep your head erect, and relax your shoulders. Think of the thing you want most in the world. Picture yourself doing or having it –

If I had to live my
life over again, I'd
dare to make more
mistakes next
time.

Nadine Sanger

as though it has happened. Make the picture and feeling as real as you possibly can. Take a few deep breaths, open your eyes, and return to whatever you are doing in a more relaxed, happier and effective state of mind.

Change History

We know we cannot change what has happened, but we can change the way we think about the past. Because it is events that have happened in the past that make us believe change is not possible in the future, it helps to alter our thinking about them. If you do this, you can also change the way you feel about your ability to succeed.

It is our experience of failing to give up a habit in the past that makes us believe any future attempt will be equally futile. But what if we change the memories of our attempts to change our habits? What follow are a number of different techniques designed to help you do this.

We once had a client who, despite hating himself, said he couldn't imagine being any different. On asking him to describe something he really enjoyed he told us, in great detail, about his hill-walking holidays. He described, almost as though he were there, looking down over a river running through a valley and seeing the farms and villages laid out below. We asked him to imagine each village along the river as representing events in a person's life. To the left was the past, the right represented the future, and the town in the middle was a turning-point at which people could choose what the towns and villages in the future would be like. On doing this

he told us that he thought the people walking into the future appeared already to have made a decision to change. They knew what had gone before and could see every future decision in the light of what had happened. 'That's the life for me,' he said.

The Life Line

- ⊘ Imagine a line laid out before you that represents your life, or the length of time you've had your habit.
- ⊘ All the instances of you doing what you no longer want to do are marked out in another colour or with flags of some kind.
- ⊘ Now imagine a special kind of sticky tape that removes unwanted behaviour.
- ⊘ Stick the tape over the coloured markings or flags on the line, and then pull it off very fast so that the tape takes the old behaviours with it.
- ⊘ Scrunch up that piece of tape into a ball and throw it as far away as you can.
- ⊘ Look back again and see the past as though you never had the behaviour.
- ⊘ All that remains are your good experiences.
- ⊘ Now go along the line again, reliving all those good memories.
- ⊘ See yourself, happy and in control.
- ⊘ Imagine your future, now, being exactly the way you want it to be.
- ⊘ You are free from your habit, and you can see yourself in the circumstances in which you would normally engage in your habit, but now doing something else.
- ⊘ Experiment with the future this gives you.

⊘ Try it on for size, this other life, the life of another you who never had the habit.

⊘ What does that person do with all the extra time and money they have?

⊘ Something brilliant and inspiring?

⊘ What's it going to be for you?

⊘ Practise being this person, just like an actor taking on a new part.

Mini Exercise

You have tremendous power in the moment you say 'no' and mean it. Remember now the last time you said 'no' with real meaning and feeling. Recall now that feeling of really knowing, of being absolutely sure. Remember it again, in as much detail as you can, and hold on to that feeling. Practise, and you will be able to remember and harness that feeling whenever you need to, and go into perhaps confrontational situations more sure of yourself and your ability to deal with them.

1   *Get into state.
2   Imagine that in each hand you have a picture: in one of a time you were tempted and lapsed into your habit, and in the other of how you wished you had dealt with that situation.
3   If you need to, see yourself from behind. Just so long as you know it is you.
4   Look at the first picture, of you lapsing.
5   You can remember clearly how wrong it all went, but come out of the memory, tone down the colour and just watch it dispassionately from a distance.

Failure is often the line of least persistence.

Zig Ziglar

6 Now switch your focus to the picture in your other hand, which shows everything going the way you want it to.

7 Put that picture on top of the other one and make it twice as big. Step inside the picture and feel how it would have been to have handled that situation in the way you would have liked.

8 Try on how it feels to remain in control of the situation, and stay with it.

9 Now throw the picture in the other hand away, again and again until you can barely remember it.

10 Whenever you remember that incident, recall it in the way you would prefer to remember it.

11 You will, by repeating this enough, convince your brain that this is what happened, and it will know how to deal with similar situations as they arise.

Fast Phobias

There are times or particular circumstances when you are especially vulnerable to falling back into your habit. 'It's break time and I must have a smoke'; 'I've been reprimanded at work so I must be useless'; 'I have so much to do today, by 5 p.m. I am going to be stressed out and exhausted.'

But can you imagine this in reverse? In other words, run in your mind the process of engaging in the habit, and then the situation that leads up to your engaging in the habit. The brain has practically no reference point for things in reverse;

even reversing a car happens forwards in time. If you can see your habit backwards, it will scramble it in the brain and make it that much more difficult ever to do again.

1   *Get into state.
2   With the times we feel vulnerable in mind, let's go to the cinema.
3   We go inside, and in the dim light decide to take seats in the front row.
4   Walking down the well-worn crimson-coloured carpet, our hands running along the brass railings, we stop to pull down the flip-up chairs and take a seat.
5   On the screen in front of us we are watching a film in which you are the star, faced with the circumstances you find difficult. As we watch, the colour is drained out and we are now watching the film in black and white.
6   After a while, let's imagine that we float out of our bodies and sit in the back row, so we can now see ourselves watching the screen, and then we do it again so that now we are sitting in the projection booth watching ourselves watching ourselves watching the film.
7   Now the film starts to play backwards and circus music begins to play.
8   The whole thing is ridiculous – not dissimilar to how those circumstances you find so difficult must now seem, and will seem if you repeatedly remember them in this way.

We once asked one of our clients, whose success at breaking a habit really impressed us, what he did whenever he felt nervous and wanted to smoke again. 'It's the funniest thing, but I saw myself in the reflection of a shop window looking nervous, and I

It's never too late to be what you might have been.
George Eliot

looked so ridiculous I laughed out loud. I didn't care what anyone thought. I just couldn't believe how funny I looked trying to fit myself back into that old nervous way of living. I just remember that,' he said.

Mini Exercise

To feel generally more relaxed, practise breathing slowly, in through your nose and out through your mouth. Take long, slow, comfortable breaths. Try counting backwards from 1,000 and, as you do so, relax every muscle in your body, starting from the top of your head and working down to your feet. Doing this once or twice a day will soon start to make a real difference in how you feel.

Making Up Memories

Many couples who are still together after more than 40 years say that to get through tough times they kept on looking for the good in each other, and never went to bed on an argument. Scientists now believe this timeless piece of advice ('Never go to bed on an argument') to have sound physiological grounding, for there is quite a lot of evidence to suggest that short-term memory takes quite a while to be encoded into long-term memory, and one of the processes that facilitates the transfer is sleep.

It is therefore possible to take control of what in the longer term you are most likely to remember. This is why children who have had potentially bad experiences with animals, such as falling off a horse, are encouraged as soon as possible to get back on and enjoy riding again. This prevents the memory of the fall becoming too ingrained, while allowing the enjoyment of being on the back of a horse to over-ride it.

One of the quickest and easiest ways to change a behaviour is to re-remember it.

When you re-remember an event or conversation or behaviour going the way you would have liked, you are setting a new direction for your life. Choose what you remember, excluding the bits that you wish hadn't been there, and you may find you behave differently next time.

A friend of ours told us about the night she was writing out her Christmas cards. As she put pen to paper on card number 71, her husband demanded to know when he would be eating supper, one young daughter wanted stories read to her, while the baby woke up and started crying. Retelling the story she was able to laugh, and we pointed out that, had she written the story of the moment into the Christmas card (Dear So-and-so, this is card no 71, husband is wingeing, daughter wants to be told stories, baby has woken and is crying. Feeling rather pissed off myself. Love, Me. P.S. Merry Christmas) there was a good chance its recipient would have laughed too, and would probably have rung her up to share what by then seemed like a good joke. By remembering the instance in this way, she was able to change the memory from a bad and rather stressful event into a rather cheerful and amusing one.

1 *Get into state.
2 Can you think of the last time you were irritated or cross about something, or ended a conversation feeling bitter or dissatisfied?
3 When you look back on it and retell the story of the event to yourself in your head, how do you feel?

4 Sometimes you can laugh at how you behaved, or think of how you might have handled the situation differently.

5 Think of the last time you lapsed in your continuing attempt to break your habit.

6 Look back at yourself from the outside and watch yourself dealing with that situation.

7 What would you do differently if you were there now, standing by and watching yourself?

8 What if you could reach out as this other you, this other person, struggles, and tickle them under the chin?

9 What happens then?

10 How do they react?

This technique can be used to change the memory of having failed in the past, or immediately after a lapse as you try to break your habit, so next time you are faced with a similar set of circumstances, your memory is not of giving in to the temptation, but of resisting it.

step 9

Getting Stronger

Making Change Happen

There is a well-known television presenter in the UK whose physical appearance changed dramatically over a number of years. This once rather frumpy young woman was transformed to such a degree that she came to be regarded as one of the most attractive in the country. While she may well have been ambitious, intelligent and cunning, she also, perhaps without even knowing, regularly practised self-belief. Many years ago, when she first began working, she had what we will call a 'mirror mantra'. Every time she looked at her reflection she would say one word to herself: 'Gorgeous'. Over subsequent years, that is exactly what she became.

That change took many weeks to manifest, but there is no rush to make change. Some people find it easier than others, while a number achieve success fairly fast. None of this matters – getting there is all that counts, and we are here to pace you through it.

Do not be desirous of having things done quickly. Do not look at small advantages. Desire to have things done quickly prevents their being done thoroughly. Looking at small advantages prevents great affairs from being accomplished.

Confucius

Power Moves

Pete writes: Some time ago I was working with a former Olympian sports medallist who, minutes before we were due to stand up to do a presentation in front of 100 people, disappeared into the Gents saying he wanted to get himself ready. This for him meant standing in a semi-crouched position, his knees bent and one foot in front of the other, shouting at the top of his voice: 'YES, YES, YES.' Others passing by outside might have wondered what was going on, but he did not care. All that concerned him was getting into the right state to give the best presentation he could.

Think of some of the professional sportspeople you might have watched on television. Many of them make what may sound to us like strange noises, or shout particular words as they hit a tennis ball or throw a football. They do this because, having practised over and over, they have come to know the result it will produce.

Recall the affirmation you wrote in the belief exercise (page 30).

Write it down again here: _____

_____

We are going to ask you to do the Future You exercise again (page 98).

This time, when you step into the future you we want you to repeat your affirmation to yourself, out loud or in your head, and at the same time do some physical movement to maximize the effect of this affirmation. Some people like to make a fist and punch the air, or draw their clenched fist back towards their waist as they would on having achieved a much sought-after goal. One friend of ours looks in the mirror, smiles, clenches his fist and says: 'Go baby, go', while another does the Can Can! It need not be that dramatic, but with practice, it will work.

Find some sort of physical movement you can do as you recite your affirmation which reinforces the feeling of 'I can'. We know that this can help you to get into a state ready for change.

Try doing it now: your own 'Power Move' should help you to feel the words in your affirmation throughout your body.

Doing this in a rather half-hearted way will not do. We need conviction.

If the words 'Power Move' sound uncomfortable for you, call it your Success Signal, or even Dave.

1   Imagine standing outside your front door.
2   The door opens and you see yourself in the future, having broken your habit.
3   You are feeling stronger, more powerful and in control.
4   Look at that you.
5   In a moment you are going to step into that you as though you were trying on how it feels.
6   As you step in, repeat the affirmation and do your Power Move or Success Signal.

DO IT NOW!
Once you have done this exercise a few times at home and are skilled at it, you can do it almost anywhere, though you don't have to say the affirmation out loud. Repetition enforces the message, so the more often you can do it, the better.

Fate somehow ensures that certain events come to pass; how they are handled it leaves to you.

A consultant friend of ours told us that he always received many accolades at the end of his group sessions, but tended to brush them off. Then one day he decided that those who complimented him must have good reason, and were probably not in the habit of lying, so he began looking in the mirror before he left for work each day playing back to his reflection some of the compliments he regularly received.

By living out the person he was told he was, his work got better, as did the commendations. When one woman once remarked on how attractive he was, he repeated the technique and within weeks dozens more women were making comments on his appearance. Believing that other people believed these things about him helped this consultant to behave as they were expecting, but to an even greater and more demonstrative extent.

From now, instead of criticizing yourself, get into the much more useful habit of beginning and ending your day by looking in the mirror and repeating your affirmation with or without your Power Move. Do it whenever you see your reflection or when you need to motivate yourself for a particular task. See what sort of a difference it makes, both to your behaviour and your attitude towards and about yourself. You are the only one who can give yourself self-confidence.

Mini Exercise

Is there someone you have watched undergo a remarkable change? It might be losing weight, changing career or just being happier. A friend of ours who began exercising underwent just such a change. His sour expression disappeared, his beer-belly started to shrink and he looked happier and more in control of his life. We all wanted to know how he had

Be curious always!
For knowledge will
not acquire you,
you must acquire
it.
Sudie Back

done it. If you know or ever meet anyone who tells of or demonstrates a similar life-changing transformation, why not ask them how they did it? Their formula may not work the same wonders for you, but it would be worth a try.

The more you
depend on forces
outside yourself,
the more you are
dominated by
them.
Harold Sherman

Circles of Confidence

What is confidence? It is a feeling, just like any other feeling, but when we feel confident, we feel good about ourselves and in control. Feelings are just chemicals that are mixed inside our brain. We want you to develop the habit of mixing your own cocktail of chemicals. Rather than automatically mixing those which induce feelings of being worried or stressed, you can learn to mix feelings of confidence or being relaxed or happy.

We find that many people need their confidence building up when trying to break a habit. Those almost inevitable times of weakness that people experience can make them feel vulnerable, and as a result they can lapse back into their old ways. This is when they need to put themselves into a resourceful state, and rise above temptation. Many do this by repeating their affirmation, or using some other exercise that helps restore their confidence.

You may think other people are more talented, luckier or happier than you, and so naturally feel more confident. Maybe some of them do have a better match between inner resources and opportunities, but most successful people have learned to draw on the positive experiences in their lives to build stronger beliefs in themselves and their ability

You must do the thing you think you cannot do.
Eleanor Roosevelt

to achieve. They also draw from negative experiences, but only to learn from them before moving on.

Is it time yet to start living the life that your old way of behaving wouldn't let you? People who succeed, who meet and then out-perform even their own expectations, tend to do things differently from their less successful peers. Hardly surprising, but most of the changes people make come almost naturally from realizing the obvious and taking action.

Taking a close look at the alternative to whatever you did in the past can be a very effective motivator. So have a good look at where your actions are taking you. If any generalization about the unwanted habits people have is true, it's that they take time and money to maintain. What will you do with the time and the money left over once your habit is gone? Choose something, and then do what you need to get it.

We believe our basic quality of life, and therefore how we feel about ourselves, comes down to how we filter what happens to us. Think about some wonderful experiences from your own life and write them down. These can be times when you felt happy and confident and were having fun. What happens when you recall these times? Do you remember the experience as though it were happening now, or do you recall the memory from a distance, as though you were watching a replay on TV?

1   Get into state.
2   Take one of those experiences now and imagine seeing it on a big screen.
3   Make it bigger, brighter, bolder, clearer and imagine the picture starts moving closer to you till it moves inside you and you step back in and relive it.
4   Repeat this with each of the positive experiences.

1   Now think of a few difficult experiences in your life –
no major issues, just times when you had to deal with
adversity or apparent failure.
2   What happens when you think about these times?
3   Are you back there in the experience, or can you watch it
from a distance?

Neither way of recalling an event is right or wrong – it is just
the difference in how we have filtered what has happened to
us that counts. We need to get some distance from the negative experiences, and move closer to the times we enjoy.

Successful people have learned how to distance themselves from uncomfortable experiences in their lives. Because
they have done this they have a great many positive experiences to draw from, and accordingly think, act and expect
positive things to happen. Many of us do the opposite and find
it hard to recall happy times. We expect things to go wrong,
like expecting to fail at breaking a habit.

1   Get into state*.
2   Imagine seeing yourself, as though on a television screen,
in the negative experience.
3   Imagine the screen gets smaller, shrinks and moves
further away.
4   Make the picture black and white and push it so far away
that it is no bigger than the head of a pin.
5   Now make it disappear.
6   Think about the experience again, and notice the
difference. It is difficult to feel the same way about it.
7   Do this as many times as you need to, to make the
process automatic.

In being able to recall happy memories, it should be clear that you know how to feel confident. You also feel this way when doing something you are good at and/or enjoy. It could be cooking, ironing, playing tennis, doing karate or dancing. What you might not know is how to harness that feeling and use it as and when you want to. This is what the next exercise will teach you to do.

1 Make a list of all the times in your life when you had a really strong, confident feeling.
2 Pick five of the best and stand up, making sure you have some space in front of you.
3 Get into state*.
4 Imagine a coloured circle in front of you, big enough for you to step into.
5 Recall one of those confident experiences in your life.
6 Imagine you can see yourself in that experience inside the circle.
7 See what you look like, sound like and feel like, watching that you.
8 When you have a strong recollection of this and are ready, step into the circle and straight back into the experience as though you are there now.
9 Relive that feeling of confidence, making the experience more alive and colourful.
10 When you have absorbed as much confidence as possible from the memory, step out of the circle.
11 Repeat this exercise again with each of the other confident experiences in your life, using your imagination to allow each event to be better than the last as you keep adding to the confidence you already experience in the circle.

STEP 9 Getting Stronger

12 When you have done it with each, step into the circle and relive the experiences again, one straight after the other.
13 Now, think of a time in the future when you will need those feelings of confidence.
14 Imagine yourself in the circle just before you need to be confident – in other words, just before you are usually triggered to fall back into your old habit.
15 As you see yourself, step into the circle and feel the confidence spreading right around your body.
16 Imagine the situation you foresee unfolding around you, with self-confidence fully available to you.
17 Step out of the circle and think about the difficult situation you face.
18 Notice how different you feel about it.

You can take this imaginary circle with you, or you could use the power of your imagination to turn the circle into a bracelet:

1 Look at the circle on the floor. Shrink it in your mind's eye.
2 Look at its bright and shiny colour.
3 Now pick it up and slip it onto your wrist.
4 Squeeze it around your wrist and, as you do so, allow the feelings of confidence that it gives off to spread throughout your body.

Whenever you need to feel confident in the future, especially before going into a situation you know might be a challenge, squeeze your imaginary bracelet, feel the confidence and deal with the situation.

In addition to this, when you experience times of feeling confident in the future, make your bracelet stronger by squeezing it and adding that feeling to it.

Mini Exercise

This is a really quick way of 'resetting' how you feel during the day, but it might mean changing the way you sit.

At the base of your spine is your pelvis, and at the bottom of your bum as you sit on a chair are two bones. Find them. Now move your centre of gravity and straighten up until you can find the point at which your body is comfortably support-ing itself with minimum effort. Your body is designed to be upright, so this can only be of benefit to you, and by learning to allow your body, and not your chair, to support you, also helps to tighten the stomach muscles.

Re-centre Your Balance (Hara)

When asked, a friend of ours said the best thing about practising martial arts was the ability and confidence it gave him to say 'no'. It gave him control of himself and the state he was in, to the point where he could not be swayed by any outside influence. In prac-tising this discipline, he was able to go into this state whenever he wanted or needed to.

Many practised martial artists are able to go into whichever state they want whenever they want. We once saw a show given by some martial artist monks who were demonstrating strength and flexibility by lying on beds of nails and doing somersaults in the air. These are people who have learned how to put their attention into the strongest part of their body: their centre.

Imagine you have a small tennis-size ball in the middle of your stomach, the strongest point in your body. Breathe into that part of your body and feel strong.

Whom do you know or admire who can stay in a resourceful state no matter what? When we are in a negative state of mind, we talk down to ourselves and our attention is all in our head. When we feel good, confident and strong, our attention is more evenly spread through our body and tends to concentrate in our centre, our stomach, making us feel much more balanced. Could you imagine the golfer Tiger Woods or the former South African President Nelson Mandela talking to themselves negatively or giving themselves a hard time when under pressure?

Get a friend to stand by you for this next exercise.

1 Stand straight up with your eyes on the horizon and your feet shoulder-width apart.
2 Now think of a time when you've felt overwhelmed or stressed, perhaps at the amount of work in front of you, or at a task you've had to complete by a particular time.
3 You no doubt felt anxious and concerned about how you were going to get through this time.
4 As you concentrate on this feeling of anxiety and stress, tell your friend to push against your upper arm just below the shoulder in an attempt to force you over.
5 You should find that you are unable to put up much resistance: your brain is too focused on your problems to divert any strength to keeping you upright.

6   Now, find the point on your lower stomach which is about three finger-width spaces below your belly-button. This is called *hara* by those who practise yoga. Press a finger on that point and, as you take your finger away, relax completely and put your attention on that point.

7   Get your friend to try to push you over again. You should find that, this time, you are much more solid.

We spend much of our time with our attention fixed in our heads, worrying mostly, and wonder why we often feel wobbly and out of control.

When you need to feel more stable or in control, or the next time you are confronted by someone putting pressure on you to revert to your old habits, or even when you have an issue you are finding difficult to tackle, just switch your focus from your mind to that point below your naval. Your ability to face whatever difficulty you confront will automatically increase.

Reminders/Anchors

A smell, a tone of voice or a piece of music are examples of things that can remind us of people, places or feelings we've had in the past. They are known as *anchors*, because they anchor us to particular events in the past. There are also anchors that can remind us of times when we performed exceptionally well or when we felt particularly able or confident.

We can create our own anchors, so that when we feel the need for extra confidence or self-control, there is a means by which we can immediately tap into it.

1 Get into state*.
2 Remember a time when you performed exceptionally.
3 Imagine the experience as though you were there now.
4 You may find it easier to concentrate on one aspect of the memory at a time.
5 The more senses you use (see it, feel it, smell it, and so on), the easier it will become to recall and relive.
6 Once you have a strong representation of the memory, mark the experience in some way (such as pressing your hands together, rubbing your eyebrow, looking at your watch or saying a phrase to yourself) so your unconscious mind knows what you want it to do when you repeat this 'mark'.
7 You need to repeat marking the memory with the action again and again until you know, just by looking at your watch or pressing your hands together, that the mark and feeling are anchored.

And Lastly ...

⊘ Ask yourself: whom would I least like to embarrass myself in front of?
⊘ Make a list of as many people as possible. (If the thought of showing yourself up in front of any of these people is more than you can bear, you've got the right people.)
⊘ Buy some postcards, and on each write a declaration stating what you will stop doing, and what you will do instead.
⊘ Send the cards to the people on your list.
⊘ Live up to it!

step 10

Taking Care of Yourself – The Habit of a Lifetime

There is only one success – to be able to spend your life in your own way.
Christopher Morely

The happiest people don't necessarily have the best of everything. They just make the best of everything.

Habits prevent us from being ourselves and really enjoying our lives. Often the habits we want to change become the walls behind which we hide, making us our own prisoner. Guarding us from escaping are our egos, which tell us: 'Don't even think about getting out and changing: it just isn't you.' Our irrational beliefs – that we cannot change because this is the way we are – act as the prison bars through which we stare. We believe that we are locked up and that there is no escape. But there is. It is just that many of us are too frightened of what we might find to try.

We have learned that success in breaking a habit does not last if we give people the skills and techniques without also offering them something to replace the habit with. We all need to take on a different habit and commit to doing something else.

The habit of a lifetime, for most of us, should be taking care of ourselves. But the majority of people, for a number of different reasons, do not know how to do this. Mainly it is because of the ways in which we have been conditioned as we have grown up, so that often the biggest habit any one of us has is not taking care of ourselves.

Pete writes: Some years ago I was suffering from exhaustion and needed to take some time off work. But I was self-employed, so I didn't. I suffered for the following four years, constantly having to take time off without ever properly recovering. Being that unwell for so long was tough, but it taught me one of the most important lessons I think I will ever learn. I had been doing what I wanted, rather than what I needed, to do. I wanted to go on working regardless, but I needed to have more fun, space, time on my own and recreation to recharge my batteries. I had forgotten how to take care of myself and knew only how to take care of others. Of course, I had let myself get into a situation where I could not take care of anyone, let alone myself. Over time I learned that the best way to help others was to help myself.

Get your notebook out now, and make a list of all the things you want. This could include a new car, a new house, a new job or a new wardrobe.

When you have done that, make another list of all the things you think you *need*. People often forget that they need fun and enjoyment as much as they need clothing – in fact, some need it even more.

One of the questions that I really enjoy asking people is what they think they will wish they had done less of once they reach the age of 90. Most commonly the responses are: 'I

The secret of success is making your vocation your vacation.

Mark Twain

wish I'd worried less' or 'I wish I had not been so negative'.

Ask yourself this question, then write the answers down in your notebook.

I always follow this question with another. When you are 90, what do you think you will wish you had done more of? People often say laughed more, travelled more or had more fun.

Answer this question yourself, writing the answer in your notebook.

You are (probably) not 90. Many people, having done this exercise, find this a huge relief. It makes them realize that the way they are now, the way they think and the things that they do are not set in stone. It is possible to change, if they really want to.

You could quite easily now say: 'Oh, well, I will change tomorrow', or 'I will wait until things in my life calm down'. But life is always full of unforeseen circumstances. There will always be other people and events trying to grab your attention. You cannot wait for the perfect time – you have to work with what you have got. Putting things off and talking yourself out of change has already robbed you of so many opportunities. You don't have to repeat that mistake again.

Doing What You Love and Loving What You Do

One of the secrets to loving your life is knowing what it is you truly love. Unfortunately, many of us are brought up learning how to concentrate instead on what we dislike.

We are probably at our happiest, devoid of destructive habits, when very small, most likely between the ages of 0 and 4. The only habits we had then were being happy and seeking to enjoy all that we did. As children we were like sponges, absorbing almost every bit of information that came our way, even though much of it was useless, pointless even, and often negative. Instructions such as, 'You must finish all the food on your plate' or 'Don't run in the house', if we think about it, served practically no useful purpose whatsoever. Often we were told not to touch something which, because we think in pictures, reinforced the desire to do just that.

Many of us grow up learning how *not* to do things. We know what we cannot do, where we cannot go and what we aren't allowed to say or even think and feel. In studies it has been found that one of the first words a child learns is 'no'. We are taught denial and, with practice over the years, we become experts, knowing everything about how to feel bad about ourselves, and barely anything about how to feel good.

Remember, humans are the newest species on the planet and, in many ways, are still evolving. We have in our make-up inbuilt imperfections, so trying to be perfect is pretty futile. Maybe you think you are too tall or too small, your nose is too big or you are too fat. Although physiologically you can change to a certain degree, that is the way you are. What you *can* change, however, is the way that you think and how you feel inside. But it takes time to change the way we have been conditioned to think about ourselves, so have patience.

How happy are you right now? Many of us know what makes others happy, but are unsure of what makes us happy. We challenge you to be willing to pursue happiness.

Make this your habit. Today you might not be so familiar with trying, but, like any other behaviour, it can be learned. Infants feel content when their most basic needs alone are met. Do you have everything you need? Go back to your list and check.

We want you to discover the habit of feeling good about yourself. For many this means sailing uncharted waters and, if you choose this path, do not expect plain sailing, because life is just not like that. Lasting changes tend to happen in increments, day by day, hour by hour, minute by minute and heartbeat by heartbeat. But what you do need on this journey is a new approach.

What follows are some simple techniques designed to help you take on board the habit of a lifetime – the habit of truly taking care of yourself.

You Are What You Think

What do you think the basic quality of your life comes down to? We believe it is defined by how well or how badly we communicate with ourselves. We are always asking ourselves questions, talking to ourselves and giving ourselves messages. The conclusions and answers we draw from these conversations help us to reach decisions about the way we live our lives. The problem is, most people ask themselves the wrong questions, such as 'Why didn't it work?', 'Why can't I do that?', 'Why don't they like me?' or 'Why did they say that?'

When trying to break a habit, we more often than not ask ourselves: 'Why can't I give up smoking/biting my nails/

procrastinating/being stressed/drinking?' The brain will only ever try to offer a helpful answer, but to get from it a far more effective and useful one we need to learn to explore our own potential to help ourselves by asking: 'What could I be doing to gain control and give up this habit?' Don't forget, what you think about is what you tend to get. You set the direction you want to take.

Most people are used to and therefore very good at giving themselves a hard time. Are you? Consider for a moment whether you would treat your best friend the way you treat yourself. Giving ourselves a hard time is probably one of the most common habits of those who live in the Western world, yet none of us was born with this habit. Babies don't do it. We learn how to analyse and criticize ourselves from others as we grow up.

Think about this: scientists estimate that the average person has between 50,000 and 60,000 thoughts a day. This means, roughly, that we have a different thought every second during a 16-hour day. Day in, day out our minds are whirring constantly with impulses, notions and urges of one sort or another in that intuitive process we call thinking.

It is said that one of the first signs of madness is talking to ourselves. If this were true, we must all be mad, because we all do it, all the time. The reason it mostly goes unnoticed, even by ourselves, is that we do it inside our heads. We say to ourselves: 'I am stupid', or 'I can't do anything properly', or 'Nobody likes me'.

Having such thoughts, for many of us, is like eating; we do it automatically, without really appreciating what is going into our bodies (or our minds). What often gets forgotten is that these thoughts, in many ways like the kinds of food we eat, shape our lives. It is helpful to take a really close look at our thoughts and change them to develop a more positive attitude.

We are where we are and what we are as a result of the thoughts that have dominated our minds. Life can so easily be thrown away on worries and guilty feelings. If unconsciously we are creating our own dramas and expecting the worst to happen, it often does. We struggle from day to day, lurching from crisis to crisis without even knowing we have a choice. It is also our thoughts that often lead us into having habits we would rather not have. If you can change your thoughts, you can change your habits.

Pay more attention to your internal dialogue and become more aware of what you say to yourself and how you treat yourself. For the next three or four days, write down all of your thoughts and the sorts of things you say to yourself. We call this process a Thought Download. It may come as a surprise what occupies your mind.

We need to learn to stop talking to ourselves all the time and just listen and observe what is happening. All too often we get so caught up in what *has* happened, what *could* happen and what *might* happen, that we miss out on what actually *is* happening. We fail to experience life.

The Chinese are well known for their ability over many thousands of years to observe their behaviour uncritically. They seem to be able to step back and watch what they do without making a judgement. Would you like to be a judge in a court, deciding whether someone is guilty or innocent? Probably not. Judging is hard work, and so is judging ourselves and others. Babies and very young children are also good at watching; they only learn to criticize from adults as they grow.

Observe without judging your own thoughts as you write them down. See this exercise as a way of gathering important information – you are a secret agent with the task of investigating the thoughts of the most important person in the world: you.

We believe it is important to be aware of what thoughts control our lives. Most people do not even question their thoughts, or consider where their thoughts might be taking them. Once you understand that your thoughts play a crucial role in the direction your life takes, you are in a position to begin learning how to control them and ultimately live the life you want.

Having written down the thoughts that occupy their minds, many people see that they spend a lot of time feeling stressed, being worried, feeling guilty and criticizing themselves. They then say: 'Why do I give myself such a hard time?' The answer is *practice*. Often our brain does not know that being kinder is a better and more positive option. It only suggests what it thinks is best and what it already knows, which invariably means doing what we have always done and being hard on ourselves.

Many of us go over and over the same habits, behaviours, worries, stresses and regrets and fill ourselves up with what's wrong with and missing from our lives. These thoughts seem to follow us round like a big, dark cloud, and at night they can rob us of sleep. This way of thinking severely limits our capacity for new and creative thoughts, and steals away from us the joy of living. Without thinking about it we can throw away every precious 24 hours that come our way.

Once you have written down your thoughts for a few days, take an overview and try to spot any patterns. Look and see

Our life is what our thoughts make of it.

Mark Aurelius

if your thoughts are helping or hindering you. If you find that many of your thoughts are not serving you, then it is time to make a new list of the kind of thoughts you would like to have that would support where you want to go in life.

Your new list might include the kind of thoughts that you think will help you to increase your skills and capabilities, complete your everyday tasks or improve your health and fitness.

You might be thinking now that the thoughts you have are impossible to turn round, but it is really very easy. For example, most people know that exercise and keeping fit are good for them, but just thinking about the effort involved in any sort of physical activity turns them off and they immediately talk themselves out of it. It is no wonder that so many people are unfit and overweight when their thoughts make exercise seem so unappealing.

A way to change your thoughts in this example is to focus on the outcome of regularly doing some sort of sport or exercise. Think about how you'll feel when you are finished – virtuous and on a natural high from the endorphins released during physical activity. You could also think about how you will feel a few weeks' or months' hence: probably slimmer, fitter, energized and happier with yourself. With that feeling, go and exercise and take the feeling with you.

Once you start practising this you will discover all sorts of new opportunities and directions that are available to you. You will realize that you can steer your life, not simply drift along.

Start to see how many new thoughts you can incorporate into your thinking day. There will be some repetition, of course, but the essence of a more fulfilling life is to start to accommodate as many new thoughts as possible. And if you find you are talking to yourself in a negative or derogatory manner, tell yourself to shut up, then give yourself some encouragement and be kind, as you would be to a child or a best friend.

Being Your Own Best Friend

Talking about best friends, who is yours? Would you ever treat them the way you treat yourself? Of course not, because if you did, they would not be your best friend any more.

We are so accustomed to being told how to live or aspiring to be like other people that we probably wouldn't know ourselves if we walked in the front door.

Practise being your own best friend and begin to know yourself, understanding and appreciating your imperfections. Whether it be a fear of heights, a dread of public speaking or nervousness around members of the opposite sex, if we can look at our hang-ups dispassionately and laugh at ourselves, we are enormously empowered to change.

Some people feel embarrassed by the idea of liking or loving themselves, and say they cannot do it. But if you strip away all your beliefs and behaviours, love is all that is left. And if you love yourself enough, you won't want to subject yourself to any kind of destructive habit. If you appreciated yourself that much more, do you think you would have unwanted habits?

Stop for a moment and consider some of the following:

Did you know that you have 15 billion brain cells?

Did you know that the average life of a tastebud is 10 days?

Did you know that you can hear 1,600 different frequencies ranging from 20 to 20,000 cycles per second?

Did you know that your eyes can detect a single photon of light?

Did you know the 800,000 fibres in each of your optic nerves transmits from 132 million rods and cones to your brain more information than the world's largest optical computer system?

Did you know that humans are capable of producing 7,000 facial expressions using 44 facial muscles?

Did you know that the 300 million air sacs in your lungs provide oxygen to the 100 trillion cells throughout your body?

Did you know that you have 206 bones and 656 muscles which form a more functionally diverse system of capabilities than any known creature?

Quite a remarkable creature, aren't you?

Most of us, though, are not brought up to love or even appreciate ourselves. When we feel uncomfortable, we often take action which numbs or blots out our feelings. This can take many forms, but as we now know, often the behaviours that numb our feelings become habits, such as drug dependency, overeating, smoking, drinking or having low self-esteem.

Because we do not love or at times even like ourselves, because we barely even know ourselves, we put up barriers of protection which often become self-destructive, and hide who we really are.

Perhaps loving something is the only starting place there is for making your life your own.
Alice Koller

We challenge you to make friends with yourself, to become your own best friend. Who do you think is the most important person in the world? Perhaps a number of people come to mind. In truth, the answer is you. If you really want to change the world and make it a better place, you need to make friends with that important person because he or she is the only person over whom you have absolute control.

The single stupidest sentence ever in the history of the English language is 'Do it right first time.' Nobody ever did anything even half interesting the 41st time.
Tom Peter

Making Mistakes and Enjoying the Struggle

You are always going to have times of struggle; that is just a part of life. But it is your ability to deal with the struggle that matters. When you know you are struggling, change your attitude towards it and say to yourself: 'I am going to enjoy this, because I will learn something from it and I know it will not last.'

Life is difficult. This is a great truth, one of the greatest truths. It is a great truth because once we truly see this truth, we transcend it. Once we truly know that life is difficult – once we truly understand and accept it – then life is no longer difficult. Because once it is accepted, the fact that life is difficult no longer matters.
M. Scott Peck

We have found that the people who get on in life and are happy are the ones who have learned from whatever happens to them. They accept that adversity and struggle are an integral part of life, and that how they handle it will make the difference between staying behind or getting ahead.

Even though we often fail to realize it, some of the most important lessons we learn are through making mistakes, and the same principle applies when we make mistakes or have setbacks when trying to change our behaviour. If you do lapse, it does not mean you have to abandon your attempts at trying to change. Learn from it, and move on. If you don't, it is likely you will repeat the mistake until you do.

What the hell – you might be right, you might be wrong ... but don't just avoid.

Katharine Hepburn

Keep changing your responses to your mistakes and you can change your life.

Dealing with Unforeseen Challenges

The block of granite which was an obstacle in the pathway of the weak, became a stepping-stone in the pathway of the strong.

Thomas Carlyle

A friend who has a highly successful career in fashion says his secret is being able to deal with the unforeseen. That is what problems are – events that we do not always make allowances for or expect. His to-do list is never done at the end of each day, he says, because he has had the unforeseen events to deal with. Rather than seeing them as problems, he makes the unforeseen a series of challenges, and deals with them in that way.

Thomas Edison, while trying to find a filament that would light the world's first lightbulb, struggled for months and made hundreds of mistakes. Every time he tried an unsuitable material, he simply took the view that he had eliminated another possibility. When asked by a journalist how he felt to have failed time after time, Edison replied that he had not failed: he had successfully found many ways that did not work. This attitude kept him motivated and positive, and he persevered until he found the solution to the challenge he faced.

Do you prefer problems or challenges in your own life? Think of a problem you have, whether it be to meet a deadline or deal with a particular person or situation.

Say to yourself: *The problem I have is* ....

....

Notice how that feels.

Now repeat this, but this time say: *The challenge I have is*

....

Notice how that feels.

You probably know, having read this far, that the words we use and the words we hear really do have an effect on the way we feel. People in general much prefer challenges to problems. Challenges do just that: they challenge us to do them. Problems are things we wish we never had to deal with.

Be aware of how often you use the word 'problem' in your life. When you next find yourself using it, stop and replace it with the word 'challenge'. You might find the idea of doing this daft or silly, but have a go.

How to Be Successful

What does being successful mean to you? When asked, a great many people will define success as being when they have achieved something or reached a particular goal. Strange, what about all the times in between? You are being successful even on the way to achieving a goal. Start being successful at being happy, and judge your success by how happy you are.

One of the secrets to doing this successfully is to love what you do and do what you love. We know this is not always easy, especially if you are in a job that you don't like or in a difficult relationship. But make a decision to enjoy what you do now, in the present, because that is what it is, a

Our deepest fear is not that we are inadequate. Our deepest fear is that we are powerful beyond measure. It is our light, not our darkness, that most frightens us. We ask ourselves, who am I to be brilliant, gorgeous, talented, and fabulous? Actually, who are you not be? You are a child of God. Your playing small doesn't serve the world. There is nothing enlightened about shrinking so that other people won't feel insecure around you. We are born to make manifest the Glory of God that is within us. It's not just in some of us, it's in everyone, and as we let our own light shine, we consciously give other people permission to do the same. As we are liberated from our own fear, our presence automatically liberates others.

Nelson Mandela

present, and it won't come round again. You are making your future now, so make the most of it.

After all, if your life is not the way you want it to be, who is responsible? Fair enough, your parents, siblings, relatives, partners, teachers and friends might have played some part, but come on, who is ultimately responsible? Are you really willing to change your life and take on new habits, or do you just think it is a nice idea? If you think it is merely a nice idea or is something you think you 'should' do, forget about it.

Watch What You Wish For

So how do any of us become what we want to be? Well, some things may come about by chance, but most of us start out by wishing. Through that wish comes an expectation, a purpose and a direction, then whatever we wish for, happens. It sounds simple, almost unbelievable, but if we look at it from another angle, we can see how wishing works.

'I wish this didn't keep happening to me.'

'I wish life wasn't so awful.'

'I wish people wouldn't keep dumping me.'

'I wish I didn't find it so difficult to find a job.'

Do any of those phrases sound familiar? Most people wish for what they *don't* want instead of thinking about what they *do* want and using their imaginations to create that possibility.

Imagining a Better You

It's a funny thing about life; if you refuse to accept anything but the best, you very often get it.

W. Somerset Maugham

Imagine what it is going to be like once you are taking better care of yourself.

Grab your notebook and write down:

– what you would be doing
– what would be different about your life
– what you would be eating
– what kind of exercise you would be taking
– how often and in what way you would be relaxing
– what you would not be doing any more
– how you would be feeling.

Whatever you can do. Or dream you can. Begin it. Boldness has genius, power and magic in it. Begin it now.

Goethe

See yourself behaving in these ways, as though you are already taking better care of yourself. You can then begin to live the dream. It really is no more difficult than that. Achieve little bits at a time, for as long as it takes. You can win in every step you take towards being kinder to yourself – and don't let anyone else, for whatever reason, pull you away from your purpose.

The thing has already taken form in my mind before I start it. The first attempts are absolutely unbearable. I say this because I want you to know that if you see something worthwhile in what I am doing, it is not by accident but because of real direction and purpose.

Vincent van Gogh

A teacher once asked his class to write a story of how they saw themselves in the future. When one boy handed in his essay which described him living on a ranch out in the country, he was given an 'F' and told by the teacher to go home and write something more realistic. Having talked about the story with his father, the boy handed the same story back in.

Sitting on his ranch 15 years later, the boy, now a man, was paid a visit by his former teacher, who said: 'You didn't let me, but I now see that I stole the dreams of a great many children. I just wanted to say that I am sorry.'

It is important to think ahead. Draw up your own plan or map of where you are going. Imagine yourself, a year from today, living a happier and more fulfilled life. What changes will you have made? How and where would you have started to make these changes? We want you to become aware that you have the resources and passion to make your dreams come true; you will not find true and lasting happiness in external stimulants or habits.

Have you ever looked in the mirror and thought, 'Who is that?' The person in the reflection looks vaguely familiar, but bears only some resemblance to the person you were expecting to be. Psychologists call this 'displacement of self', and some people go through life never recognizing or connecting with themselves.

The power to be who you want lies beneath your bills, your job, the washing up and any other difficulty you might have in your daily life. It may seem well hidden, but it is there. There is no longer any need to live life as though it were a dress rehearsal for something better. You can become today the leading man or lady of your own life.

The Habit of Taking Care of Yourself

What is the most powerful force on the planet? Love.

To take care of yourself, you need to nourish yourself, and nourishment can take many different forms. First, we believe, nourishment comes through love. It is the most powerful force on Earth, even though science cannot prove that it exists. Comfort is another dimension of nourishment, whether it be physical, emotional or mental. And so, of course, is diet.

Other sources of nourishment are the elements: the water we drink, the air we breathe, heat from the sun and the many foods we eat that owe their existence to being grown in the earth. Without any of these elements, we would be dead. The elements make life the way it is. Many of us forget what a wonderful world this is and what a great chance life can be.

We would urge you to get outside whenever you can to appreciate the most basic things in life such as a sunset or a river flowing or wind blowing through the trees. Enjoying peace and space is nourishment. We are so bombarded with information about how we should be or how we should think that we don't have time for either. Even those of us who dislike being alone need, at some point, time in our own space where we can stop doing and begin being. It is why we go on holiday.

We like to call it 'learning to become a human *being* again, instead of a human *doing*'. By being instead of doing, you can actually be in everything you do. It is the reason the very successful reach the top: they live for every minute, they are there for every minute, and they enjoy every minute of what they do. Their being is in their doing.

Another aspect of taking care of and nourishing yourself is to get back in touch with your inbuilt natural self-regulators. Intuition is one. It tells us, for example, when to eat, sleep or just relax.

Most people try to satisfy a need for nourishment externally: by drinking, smoking, eating and so on. But the best possible sensation of nourishment you can give yourself is by learning to feel good. If you can get to the point at which

Be realistic: Plan
for a miracle.
*Bhagwan Shree
Rajneesh*

The winds of grace
blow all the time.
All we need to do
is set our sails.
Ramakrishna

you don't really need any sort of stimulus to feel good, you will appreciate compliments, love, gifts – or anything else that gives you that feel-good factor – that much more.

We believe a lack of the ability to have natural self-esteem is the reason many relationships break down. Unless you are self-sufficient in the way you feel about yourself, you will be constantly expecting to be satisfied by someone else. This is artificial and will not work.

You may still think you're unworthy of any sort of happiness, success or nourishment – and perhaps to a certain extent you are right, because you have convinced yourself that this is the way you are. But it doesn't have to be that way. Whatever has happened to you in the past need not cloud or colour your future. Your life can change, and it can change for the better.

Are you resigned to staying in your prison, peering through the bars of your irrational beliefs, or have you made a real decision to change? Perhaps you have changed, but unless the gap made in your life by whichever habit you had is plugged, you could slide back into it or find another. It is only by taking on habits that really do nourish us that we are able to be successful at breaking destructive habits and be happy.

Taking care of yourself, no matter what the apparent difficulties and what your circumstances, is really the only habit you need to have. The excuses you have for not looking after yourself – family, work or other commitments – however valid they may seem, are merely part of the challenge. Focusing on your difficulties is not going to help you change, nor is continuing to believe (just because you have been repeatedly told so) that doing whatever you want to do is going to be difficult. Find a way to change, and if you can't, make one.

Observed by a trainee supply teacher, the teacher of a primary school class asked her pupils to write down a list of all the things they thought they could not do: 'I cannot sing', 'I cannot do maths', 'I cannot dance', 'I cannot learn poetry', 'I cannot run fast', and so on. To the bafflement of the supply teacher, the children were then asked to put their lists into a shoe box at the front of the class. Holding the shoe box, the teacher then led the class into the playground where they dug a little grave for it, marking it with a sign that read: 'I cannot, RIP.' A photograph of the gravestone was kept on the front wall of the classroom, and every time a child said 'I cannot' the teacher pointed to it.

You could regard this approach to change as making your own rules, which, at its most basic, is creating the rules of a new way of life. We want you to form a set of rules for taking care of yourself. You can do this in any way you want, so long as you feel good and you are being nourished by it.

We want you to have yourself – in other words, to like and love yourself. It is the biggest challenge that anyone will ever throw at you. If you take this challenge and commit yourself to it, life can become wonderful. If you can be open to the fact you can change, you can do so much more than you are doing today.

Slowing Down

We seem to live life at an incredibly high speed, trying to cram all that we believe we need to do into a day. This is despite using any number of devices to help us save time and get on with what needs to be done. What do people do with the time they save? No time is saved, really; it just tends to get filled up with more 'doing'. There is still no time for stillness, for enjoying each moment.

Babies are brilliant at this. They do not mope for hours because their favourite toy was taken away, or worry and stress about where their next meal is coming from. As soon as an unpleasant event is over, they forget about it and they never fret about what might happen tomorrow. Most of us could do with relearning this and spend some time slowing down, relaxing, recharging our batteries and being in the present moment.

Some of the most priceless memories people have come from experiencing such oneness with a moment. Can you remember any such examples? The moment at a wedding when the smiling bride walked down the aisle; watching a glowing sunset on a beach; seeing a beautiful painting for the first time; seeing a young child experience Christmas morning; being gripped by the cliff-hanger in a film or a book; or being with close friends on a once-in-a-lifetime holiday. The common thread running through all such examples is our being in the moment and not thinking about anything else, talking to ourselves or giving ourselves a hard time.

Be Responsible for Your State

Thoughts and emotions are extremely powerful. When you are angry, upset or depressed about something while around other people, they can feel it. Is that fair on them? Think how much better everyone feels if you are in a better mood or state. Emotions cannot be ignored or banished, but we can learn to control them, and if you can learn to have more control over your own state, you will be less easily influenced by others' negative states and may even be able to help them change theirs.

Learning to Slow Down – The Importance of Breath

Oxygen is the foundation of life; without it we die. Many of us breathe through our mouths, which does not properly filter the carbon dioxide. Stress, digestive and weight problems are often made worse by incorrect breathing, often no deeper than the chest. What happens if we breathe in this way? We hyperventilate, and so send a message to the body that we are constantly in a state of emergency.

You may well think you have had a lifetime's worth of practice, but as anyone who has either theatrical or medical training will tell you, the more easily you allow air in and out of your body, the easier it will be for your brain and your body to function.

One of the most natural ways to relax and slow down is to breathe. Often people say smoking relaxes them, but given that there are around 2,000 different toxic chemicals in ciga-rettes, it is more likely that the act of taking a deep breath is what is helping them to relax.

- Stop for a minute, now.
- Sit comfortably.
- Take three deep breaths.
- Allow the second and third breath to be deeper than those before.
- Just notice what happens.

Slow, deep breathing makes you more relaxed. When people are anxious, worried or stressed, their breathing tends to be short and shallow into the chest, rather than deep and incor-porating the whole diaphragm. It may be hard for some to accept, but making a simple, subtle change to the way you breathe can have a profound impact on your state.

To get an even greater benefit from this breathing exer-cise, imagine watching yourself, so you can follow the breath as you inhale and exhale. Say 'relax' to yourself as you breathe out through your mouth and in through your nose. Try to practise this breathing exercise often, when you are on the way to work or listening on the phone to someone. The more you practise, the easier it will be to repeat when you need to at a time of stress or anxiety.

Gratitude unlocks the fullness of life. It turns what we have into enough, and more.
Melody Beattie

Attitude of Gratitude

A wealthy man decided one day to take his son to the home of a poor family so he could see how they lived. After spending a day and night in the farmhouse of this impoverished family, the man asked his son what he had learned. 'I saw that we have one dog and they have four. We have a pool in the garden and they have a creek with no end. I saw that we have imported lamps in the yard while they have the stars, and while our patio covers an acre they have the whole horizon. Thanks dad, for showing me how poor we are.'

Start being more aware of what you do have in life, and focus on the things you can be grateful for. Like passion and love, gratitude is a powerful emotion. Think about a time when you were really grateful for something. Would you agree that it is a feeling that fills you up? Be grateful for each day. See it as a gift.

The Powerful Emotions Exercise

- Take a few deep breaths.
- Get comfy and, if it feels easier, close your eyes.
- Think of all the things in your life you can be truly grateful for.
- You have two arms and legs, a home, healthy children, a job. You can feel grateful for places visited, for friends and family.
- Relive the experiences or focus on the things you are grateful for having.

Dance like no one is watching. Love like you'll never be hurt. Sing like no one is listening. Live like it's heaven on earth.

William Purkey

Nothing comes from doing nothing.

William Shakespeare

The great end of learning is not knowledge but action.

Peter Honey

– Imagine yourself filling up with all the gratitude you have.

– Now think of all the things you feel passionate about. Doing the best for your children and friends, hobbies or other recreational pastimes, being involved with good causes or doing your job well.

– Go through and relive all these things.

– Imagine yourself filling up with all that passion and add it on top of the gratitude.

– Think now about all the things you love – friends, parents, pets, music, art, poetry, sport, and so on.

– See all these things, hear and feel them as you add the love to the passion and gratitude you feel and completely fill yourself up with these emotions all the way down to your toes, up to your nose and down to both hands.

– Having filled yourself up with these emotions, take a few deep breaths and bring your attention back into the room. Open your eyes and feel alert and full of gratitude, passion and love.

Conclusion

Having read this book and completed some of the exercises, you might feel inspired, enlightened and hopefully had a good laugh, but are you going to change? It is very easy now to think: 'Yes, that was an interesting book,' and go back to the way you were before.

All that changing means, in truth, is taking better care of yourself, and most people find it difficult because it is

Knowing others is intelligence; knowing yourself is true wisdom. Mastering others is strength; mastering yourself is true power.
Lao-Tzu

Follow your bliss.
Joseph Campbell

something they have never been taught how to do. You are probably great at taking care of others, but you would be even better at it if you looked after yourself first.

Pete writes: When I was younger I went out to Hong Kong to teach English. I hated it. I was there during the rainy season, staying in the most awful accommodation infested with cockroaches, and decided to phone my mum to say I wanted to come home. The first thing she said to me was: 'What about everyone else? You are letting them down.' All my life it was like that, being made to think first about other people, instead of myself. Each of us has only got one go at getting life right, and we are not going to be helping ourselves if we don't give our own lives some serious attention.

We like to use the analogy of a cup to help people get some idea of how they feel about the attention they pay to their own lives. In terms of how you feel right now, how full is your own cup? In few cases will the contents be anywhere near the top. So, if your cup is only half full, stop giving what's left in it away. If you don't, you will run out.

Instead, start filling it up to the top with what makes you happy. You have the resources, and you now know how, and can allow the journey you know you were destined to take begin any time. How long it takes and how full you can make that cup is entirely up to you. If not you, who? If not now, when?

References

J. Adams, *Motor Learning and Retention* (New York:
    Macmillan, 1977)

Susan Bay Breathnack, *Simple Abundance, A daybook of
    Comfort & Joy* (Bantam Books, 1998)

Eileen Campbell, *A Dancing Star* (Aquarian Press, 1991)

John Cornwell, 'Trick or treatment?', *The Sunday Times
    Magazine*, December 24, 2000

P. S. Erikson *et al.*, 'Neurogenesis in the adult human
    hippocampus', *Nature Medicine* 4:1313-7, November
    1998

E. R. Guthrie, *The Psychology of Learning* (New York: Harper
    & Row, 1952)

Susan Hayward, *Begin It Now* (In-Tune Books, 1991)

—, *A Guide for the Advanced Soul* (In-Tune Books, 1988)

C. L. Hull, *Principles of Behaviour* (Prentice-Hall, 1943)

'Notebook Challenging Fate', *The Scientist* 12 [22]: 35,
    November 9, 1998

A. J. S. Rayl, 'Research Turns Another Fact into Myth',
    The Scientist 13 [4]:16, February 15, 1999

Peter Silverton, 'Mind over matter', *The Observer Magazine*,
    December 31, 2000

Anne Woodharn, 'How to take comfort from a placebo',
    The Times, November 14, 2000

Resources

To find out more about Habit-busting, or if you are interested in working with one of our one-to-one Habit-busters, please visit our website at:

www.Habitbusting.com
or email at:
info@Habitbusting.com
You can also write to us at:
Habit Busting
PO Box 30887
London
W10 4WA

To find out about the Lighten Up Weight Loss Programme
    and receive a free information pack, visit our website at:
www.Lightenup.co.uk
or email at:
info@lightenup.co.uk
or ring 0845 603 3456 (calls from within the UK charged at
    local rate)
And if all of this has made you feel it's time to change your
    worklife for good, visit the website:
    www.interviewease.net

Index

Tony Buzan

Head First!

You're smarter than you think

Did you know that you only use 1% of your brain? In Head First, Tony Buzan, the foremost expert on creativity and the brain and the inventor of Mind Maps, shows you how to tap into the rest.

Did you know that you have 10 different intelligences, each one more powerful and capable of development than you ever imagined? In Head First, Tony Buzan, the world's leading expert on learning and the brain, proves that you are smarter than you think.

In 10 easy-to-follow chapters, Tony Buzan will take you through each of the 10 intelligences, which include verbal, physical, interpersonal, creative and sexual. Buzan will show you how to be brilliant with words, physically fit and more sensual, as well as how to be more in control of your time and in tune with your environment. With practical exercises and simple techniques, you will learn how to immediately enhance your ability to excel in social, personal and professional situations. Learning how to use your 10 intelligences will dramatically improve your life.